St. Louis Community College

Library

5801 Wilson Avenue
St. Louis, Missouri 63110

So You Want to Open a Restaurant

Making Your Favorite Fantasy Real

Charles Robbins

KAMPMANN AND CO.

For information contact Kampmann & Company,
9 East 40th Street, New York, N.Y. 10016.

Copyeditor: Linda Gunnarson
Composition and internal design: Dharma Press
Cover design: Lynn Hollyn Associates
Printed and bound by Fairfield Graphics

ISBN 0-93662-36-8

Printed in the United States of America.

To my mother

Acknowledgements

Several people provided generous help with this book. Special thanks are due Robert Henn and Van Bagley for their invaluable suggestions, to Ross Button and Les Horton for their unselfish gift of time, and to Perry Butler for teaching me about the restaurant business.

To Lawrence Lee for his idea and to Bill Alexander for his confidence. To Mary Bert Smyth at the Alice Statler Library, City College of San Francisco.

For their quiet contributions, my thanks to Richard Bellamy, Phyllis Bostick, and Don and Sally Schmitt

To those people in the restaurant business throughout the United States who gave freely of their energy and time and whose observations about this mad business are an important part of this book.

And to my wife for her faith and love.

Contents

Introduction

You may be in real trouble. If the thought of opening a restaurant has flitted across your mind at least once, you are marked as someone given to dreamy imaginings and to attacks of improbable fantasies. No doubt that is what your staid friends and careful advisors will tell you. Inevitably, you will have heard the horror stories about financial disaster, family destruction, and individual catastrophe. They may all be true. Ignore them.

For the other tales are also valid, those about people earning decent, fulfilling livings in restaurants. They work in their own style, must please only themselves, and are subject not to the whimsical demands of others but to their inner drive for excellence and integrity. Only a handful of restaurateurs are wildly successful. Some few become media stars. Most achieve the contentment and satisfaction resulting from worthwhile individual effort.

A restaurant is an expression of individuality, a dream made concrete. Its success can be analyzed by accountants, legalized by attorneys, explained by critics, but a good restaurant is fundamentally an idea, a sum of tiny details become a dynamic organism, a manifestation of thought and desire. It can also be a fine source of income, a fact not to be slighted.

People love food and restaurants. They enjoy eating, talking about what they have eaten, discussing new places to eat, and being within the secure walls of eating establishments. And many people who like food and like to cook have entertained the idea of opening their own place. To those who eat out frequently, almost all restaurants eventually begin to exhibit oversights and lapses. The more people know about food, the more inclined they are to want a place which will be an expression of their ideas about food.

Like a love affair maturing over the years, people's enchantment with food makes them increasingly attuned to the joys of eating and more desirous of imparting that joy to others. So they build a restaurant. And like a marriage, that restaurant can be the end of a beautiful affair. The dirty laundry room, the greasy kitchen, the complaints, and the bills are deadly and can quickly deflate the most ardent of lovers.

Yet the marriage and the restaurant can often be a means of strengthening and broadening our understanding of ourselves. The restaurant need not be all drudgery, with failure the only reward. After all, by taking a gamble on the business, you are making a personal commitment to yourself and to your future. You are attempting to earn a living by devoting yourself to that which you love. Merely by making the effort, you are beginning a process which can be immensely rewarding to you.

For almost ten years I worked in the restaurant business. During that time I met several dreamers who wanted to open their own place. Unfortunately, most lacked the knowledge and the money. Building and operating a restaurant can appear more complex and difficult to comprehend than a politician's motives. To the uninitiated, the details of restaurant operations have the appearance of a Defense Department budget, a diabolical maze with no clear direction, many dead ends, and too many costs.

In fact, restaurants, like all businesses, can be explained. Although they are certainly complicated, they do not require initiation into the black arts to grasp their workings. The difficult part is to apply your knowledge intelligently and to good effect. This book is intended to help you with the physical aspects of the procedure. In these pages you will discover a little theory and many practical hints. There are no secret recipes and definitely no magic sources of financing. There is a basic assumption that you enjoy food and people.

The restaurant business has always fascinated me. There is a constant demand for good, well-run operations. With the help of Grandpa's money, a comfortable trust fund, or a trusting banker, many people are opening their own places.

What many of those eager restaurateurs don't realize is that cash, energy, good ideas, and a few weeks spent working as a summer waiter on the Cape do not necessarily qualify them as restaurant operators. Few of us think that because we can drive an automobile we could qualify as world-class race-car drivers. But many former waiters, gourmet cooking school graduates, and otherwise sound people think that preparing a perfect fried egg for a patient spouse at home can be no more difficult than feeding twenty or thirty hungry people who have to get to work before the boss arrives and who have distressingly individual tastes in food.

There is no time for a leisurely read of the Sunday newspaper when you have several orders for eggs, all to be cooked differently, with varying requests for meats and toast (white, wheat, rye, or muffin; buttered or plain). The easygoing family member who sets a table for two in the sunny breakfast nook at home may be transformed into a naked nerve when the new restaurant coffee maker breaks, the heat lamps haven't been turned on, and the dishwasher has to be taken to the hospital during the morning rush because he just sliced his wrist on a piece of broken glass.

Of course, there is no average or typical restaurant owner. But there are certain personality characteristics that seem necessary for entry into this crazed profession. The first is ego.

Ask almost any restaurant operator about his or her reasons for opening a place, and high on the list will be an intense desire for self-expression, rooted in a very strong sense of self. All of them will say they thought they could do it better, whether they were working for a boss who didn't appreciate their work, or simply wanted the identity derived from having their own place; some may even say they like to cook.

There is no denying the rush of gratification that comes from walking into a crowded restaurant dining room, a room you have created, to be greeted by nods and waves of acknowledgment from satisfied customers. It's good for your self-image. It's not so good to walk into your dining room and be greeted by a single soup-sipper who may not have the cash for the meal and to see the wave of defiance from the bill collector peeking in through the window.

There are other personal characteristics important to a restaurant owner. You don't have to like people, but it helps. It is an industry based first on humans, then on everything else. If people are a source of irritation to you, consider becoming a sheepherder or hiring a good manager.

In thinking about the personality traits desirable in a restaurateur, I came up with the following brief profile: An aspiring restaurateur should be a self-starter with strong nerves who is decisive, organized, and optimistic. It might be noted that these are characteristics required of anyone contemplating opening a small business. If you have these traits, go ahead, start a dry-cleaning operation. But if you are thinking about a restaurant, please also ask yourself if you are interested in food. Now, I'm not saying it's impossible for someone who doesn't like food to get into the business, but unless you intend to be an absentee owner, you should have at least a passing acquaintance with food.

Since it is perishable, food requires special handling and attention. It's almost always sold in a form different from that in which it was purchased. Your customers will know what their meals are supposed to taste like—and they had better taste that way, day in, day out, every year, or you won't have customers. Yes, you need the traditional Chamber of Commerce virtues, but beyond that you need an awareness and a liking for your product and an ability to adjust to people's peculiarities.

We're not talking solid objects, like hammers and nails, which don't wear out while on the display shelf and which normally are not subjected to highly personal judgments by the people who use them. We're talking about a product that does not store well. If you order incorrectly, you won't have just one rotten pear or two; you'll have lots of waste, a lot of disappearing money, and some real headaches. If a menu item isn't properly made, you'll soon be losing customers.

Before peering into your savings book, before calling your local banker to check on the prime rate, and certainly before signing the lease on that old building that needs only a little work, stop and think. You are going into the restaurant business—and, to state the obvious, the purpose of a restaurant is to serve food. Unfortunately, many restaurant owners seem to forget this simple principle. They think gimmicky decor or plunging necklines on the waitresses will disguise the fact that their food is awful.

American eaters are becoming more astute in their evaluation of food. They buy cookbooks, read restaurant critics, and know more and more about the way food should be handled. As Patricia Unterman, restaurant writer for the *San Francisco Chronicle*, has observed, "My God, we spend more time eating than anything else except sleeping. It should be good."

When you think about your restaurant, are you thinking about food and how to make it and serve it, or about how you can use all those old pieces of junk in your garage to decorate your place? Are you planning the flow of food from kitchen to dining room, or is your mind fixed on the new clothes you will need to match the gold-flecked wallpaper in your new office?

Michael McCourt is a bartender. During the early 1960s, he owned his own place in New York City. Later he worked at Chez

Jay's in Santa Monica, California. Since 1969 Michael has been in San Francisco. He has seen many restaurants and many owners. He's not always impressed. "Humphrey Bogart and the film *Casablanca* have made more [insert an uncomplimentary epithet] get into the business. They think if they smile with a cigarette in their mouth and say, 'Play it again, Sam,' the place will fill up."

Restaurateurs who do well have a clear idea of what they want their restaurants to be. Think of the people you know and imagine trying to create a place that pleases all of them. Many will share your tastes, but others might well enjoy pastimes better practiced behind curtains. It becomes clear that you cannot please everyone. However, if you can create a restaurant pleasing to yourself, one that embodies your best ideas, then you will be one step nearer an appreciation of the benefits of working for yourself.

This book is intended to ease your way from the early planning stages, when every piece of equipment looks the same, to the weeks after opening, when reading the latest tax bill makes you doubt your comprehension of English. Unless you've worked in a restaurant, you'll never believe the number of details requiring daily attention. Many of these items will be discussed, some will be alluded to, some you will discover yourself—I hope not unpleasantly—as your place grows.

Perry Butler, owner of Perry's in San Francisco, had spent many years as an observant restaurant diner before he and his first wife opened their own place. The Butlers had constantly discussed what they liked or disliked about each establishment. By elimination and selection, they had refined the idea for their own restaurant. Perry recalls some of those meals: "We found shortcomings in almost every restaurant, and we asked ourselves why that had to be. We liked a couple of places in New York, so we knew what we wanted to do in San Francisco."

Perry's wife was an excellent cook, and their restaurant quickly established a reputation as a place to eat good food. Perry describes the fare as "saloon food" or "bar-and-grill food." He emphasizes that it is not fancy, but good, made to order with fresh ingredients.

Now, if you think that making good, basic food in a restaurant is a snap, think back on the number of poor meals you've suffered through, even when you ordered nothing more exotic than a hamburger. Perry and his wife had an idea for a restaurant serving good food and good drinks in a comfortable atmosphere. Before they talked to a real estate agent, a banker, a contractor, or a candlestick maker, they knew what they wanted.

The same can be said of men like Claude and Pierre Cappelle, who own two fine restaurants. Speaking of the way in which they planned their first place, Claude says, "We were in the wine business and going out to lunch almost every day. We always were looking for a good place to go." The brothers were raised in France and deplored the fact that there were "no places like you find in Europe, a neighborhood bistro." Le Central, their first venture, captures the solid, refined air of a Paris cafe.

The idea is the essence. You will find that creating a restaurant is not a linear affair, not a series of sequential steps, but a circle. In fact, you'll often think you're moving in circles. A spinning head is just part of the new restaurateur's normal characteristics.

As you begin to examine your idea more closely, you will become surer of exactly how the food, the decor, and the atmosphere of your restaurant will reflect your personality. The more complete and thorough your early thinking, the better grasp you will have of the project.

One of your first decisions will be how to interpret the information in this book. You must understand that there are no hard rules for opening a restaurant. The traditional choices—the right way, the wrong way, and "my way"—do not apply to restaurants or restaurateurs. There are too many variables. The customers, financial considerations, and location of Bruce's Truck Stop in Kansas won't have much in common with those of Rocky's Deli in the

Bronx. But one thing both owners will have to do is serve their patrons food without going broke in the process.

Although it is fairly evident that physical considerations can vary enormously, it is not so clear to many new operators that professional advice may vary just as much. Your accountant will tell you one thing; your spouse's accountant has a different opinion. Your partner's attorney says you have to do it his way; yours says the guy doesn't have a clue. One equipment salesman swears his stove is the best; your chef says it's a piece of junk.

So remember—no matter what kind of professional advice you receive—if you're the person who signs the checks, you're the one who's going to have to make the decisions. When I was typing the rough copy for this chapter, I made a typographical error that my wife charitably called a "psychological error." I had wanted to describe restaurant owners as needing "strong nerves." Instead, I typed "strong nevers." I was right with the latter phrase. You will have to say no many times to salespeople, employees, financial advisors, and yourself when you want to bag the whole deal and go to work for a large corporation.

You will be forced to make innumerable daily decisions that directly affect the restaurant's solvency and your own mental health. You also will be involved in many projects that interest you not at all. I have yet to meet an owner who had an equal interest in every aspect of the operation. Some people enjoy meeting the customers but hate accounting; others like to cook but are blind to the necessities of inventory control. This condition is not unique to restaurant owners.

In keeping with my belief that food is the primary concern of the restaurant business, we will discuss menu planning first. When the complexities of menu selection and organizing have been analyzed, the equally complex and no less intricate questions of location, design, and financing can be approached. And since I believe the staff of a restaurant is no less important than its food, I have included a rather detailed chapter on hiring and supervision. Finally, to keep you from relaxing under the mistaken belief that to have opened your doors to the public is to be finished with the work, we will discuss the daily food and liquor operations of restaurants.

While you are still in the conceptual stages of your restaurant project, it's a good idea to examine the impact opening a restaurant will have on your life. If you are very wealthy and can hire a chef, several managers, and all the other help you need, your new place probably will not greatly change your life. On the other hand, if you intend to be working yourself, and if you intend to serve more than tea and crumpets from two until four in the afternoon, then be prepared for decisive alterations in your life.

To say that your life will change may be stating the obvious, yet not everyone understands the time demands created by a restaurant. Le Central, owned by the Cappelle brothers since 1974, still takes huge hunks of their time. Claude says, "The work we do is responsible for our success, but the worst part of the business is the hours we put in."

Eddie Massarweh owns a 700-square-foot breakfast and lunch place. Although he has been open since 1976, he continues to work six days each week in his 50-square-foot kitchen. He smiles as he remembers the early struggles: "During the first two years it was rough. I would have sold the place for half of what I paid for it." It was four years before Eddie could afford a dishwashing machine. Now, however, he thinks that the business will continue to improve. And he knows he'll have to be there almost every morning at six to insure its growth.

You and your family will see less of each other, unless, of course, everyone works in the restaurant. In that case, you may begin to see too much of one another and too little of everyone's better side.

If you have a partner, you will have someone to share the long hours and constant problems. You also will have someone to argue with, to find fault with, to disagree with. If your partner is your spouse, you will find that a new business can strain even a solid marriage. Decisions about the way to cook the pasta, the color to paint the walls, the shape of the salt shaker, the hours of operation, or the duties of the janitor are endless and subject to the uncontrollable forces of personal opinion.

There you are, a self-motivated, decisive individual, willing to take the financial risk inherent in opening a restaurant; yet every move you make will have to be checked with your partner or spouse. For the independent type, this can be maddening.

On the other hand, because decisions required of a restaurateur often relate to questions for which there are no absolutely correct answers, the chance to discuss problems with a working partner or other interested party often helps to clarify issues.

You will find, too, that in addition to the time demands of the physical plant, your employees and customers will take their daily toll. No matter how conscientious the staff, nor how pleasant the clientele, you undoubtedly will be mentally and emotionally drained after hours of smiling and joking and being genial. You will have problems, but you cannot take them to your restaurant. Your employees won't be interested, and your customers have their own worries. In fact, one reason people will be eating at your restaurant is to avoid the complexities lurking outside.

Even if you think you are prepared to commit your time and energy and money to the project, you still may not be ready. You must be able to evaluate your knowledge of the business—and sometimes that's not easy to do. Although opening a restaurant can be more deadly than flying a small plane, there is no national licensing board to issue you a learner's permit, confirm you qualifications, or set standards that enable you to estimate your level of preparedness.

Without prior experience in the food or beverage industry, a new restaurant operator will not necessarily fail. But you won't be making things any easier on yourself. Actually, not having worked in a restaurant may be an advantage—if you have imagination and creative energy to make your place exactly what you want. However, you won't be smiling so easily if you've never been confronted by a customer whose salad is garnished with a plump, lively worm or by a kitchen with a dozen orders needing to be cooked and a refrigerator that is colder and more barren than the tax man's eyes.

You can't know *all* the answers. But if you don't have a good business background, if you don't have any idea how to schedule the prep work in a kitchen or how to organize the busperson's time, then I suggest that you initially may have to hire someone who knows more than you do. Naturally, that can create a whole new set of difficulties.

Before you spend a great deal of money, therefore, take a look at your qualifications: Do you understand quantity cooking, table service, intelligent inventory control, scheduling, and wine and beverage service? Your investment will not be a joke. Spoiled food, sloppy service, disheartened employees, and late loan payments are not funny. If you intend to have a small coffee shop, your problems will be less massive than those inherent in a 200-seat restaurant, but they will be no less important to you, nor less costly to your budget.

There are several ways to gain experience if you don't have it and don't want to hire someone who has. The most obvious is to work in another restaurant. Unfortunately, if you're not careful, you may end up making your own place much like the one in which you learned the business. Then, too, if you're mature enough to be thinking about opening a restaurant, you already may be beyond the point where introductory restaurant employment is practical or useful. It may be more instructive to dine out often, remaining continually alert to all aspects of the business.

Many high schools, vocational schools, and colleges offer courses on food service. Again, judicious observation and selection can help you tailor a program to your precise needs. Even if you don't enroll in a course, check out school and public libraries for books on the subject.

Another means of avoiding the pitfalls inherent in a new restaurant is to open a franchise operation. Generally, franchise restaurants have a better chance to survive than independently owned establishments, and the franchising company will often provide training and supervisory help to the new owner. In return, the franchisee usually pays the company a fee as well as monthly royalties.

Before signing with a franchise company, investigate it thoroughly and have your attorney examine the franchise agreement. There are several books devoted to franchising. I have listed a couple in Appendix C. Be as careful about all aspects of a franchising agreement as you could be if opening a place by yourself.

Many of your friends are going to say, "Look, dummy, with all that money in your hands, why a restaurant? Why not a good, safe money-market fund?"

Don't be swayed. Remember your ego. The desire for your own restaurant is a desire not simply for money. A restaurant is a statement of personality, an expression of your view of the world. It is a means of earning a living that requires hard work but less compromise than many jobs. A restaurant serving good food at fair prices is a gift of civilized fellowship to the community, a meeting place, a source of nourishment, a center for socializing, a refuge from the knocks and blows and indignities of the outside world. A good restaurant is a reflection of its owner's spirit and a source of joy for its customers.

1

The Menu

Restaurants are food. Behind the glitter of an opulent dining room or the functional starkness of a lunch counter are raw products that must be transformed into appealing, appetizing food dishes. Although, as owner of a restaurant, you naturally will be concerned with all types of managerial problems from personnel scheduling to uninvited cockroach conventions, your primary concern is food, a substance of endless variety and fascination, a product requiring patience and delicacy, an element at once physical and spiritual.

Food makes your restaurant. Though it may be your charming personality or the theme of your place that first attracts customers, it is the appeal of your food that will keep them returning. The connection between you and the customer is food. While other aspects of the restaurant are important, and although each patron may have chosen your place for a variety of reasons, your food—its quality, diversity, and consistency—will be the primary attraction.

Planning the Menu

An expression of your personality and professional abilities, food defines your restaurant and your attitude toward customers. Your menu is a dynamic, variable organism to be carefully considered each day, not something you simply plan, execute, and then forget at the design stage.

The menu must balance, on one side, the proprietor's dreams and talents and, on the opposite side, the community's standards and needs. Only you, as the owner, can assess your desires and ideas and then fit those into the fabric of your town or neighborhood. Knowing what you are capable of doing facilitates the planning of what you will do.

Before you begin to think about anything else, you must begin to consider your menu. For the shape, the variety, the style of your food are the major determinants in your restaurant. The menu is the touchstone, the source, from which all other concepts flow. It determines the type of service, volume of sales, investment and design, space allocations, equipment selection, purchasing methods, and your profits and success.

The impact of food on the design of the restaurant and on the people in the restaurant is similar to that of a stone thrown to the center of a pool: The rings of influence surge outward, washing over everything; when they strike the shore, they return, flowing back to the center—to the menu.

Consider the menu, therefore, as a growing entity whose birth you will control and whose development will continue as long as the restaurant continues, always maturing and improving with age. If you aren't willing to think this creatively and carefully about your main product, perhaps you shouldn't be thinking about a restaurant.

Of course, the menu does not exist imperiously alone. Every facet of restaurant design is as interwoven with the others as the threads connecting government and business. You cannot change one without altering others. While it is being planned to fit into the restaurant operations, the menu also must conform to the perceived tastes of the clientele, their habits and dining routines.

Naturally, you will have to adapt the menu to your location. When John Ash and his associate, Don Baumhefner, conceived their present operation in Santa Rosa, California, they did not envision a traditional restaurant. Instead, they wanted to build a wonderful kitchen to prepare excellent take-out food. However, when they found a suitable location—a building that previously had housed another restaurant—they completely altered their plans.

By utilizing the existing equipment, the two men created John Ash & Company, a restaurant that has been so successful in their community that they've had no time to begin the take-out operation. Even their attempts to increase their catering business have been slowed by the incessant demands of the daily restaurant business.

As you begin to refine your menu ideas, you will be concerned with certain fundamental requirements. The range and number of food selections will be a function of your own or your chef's cooking abilities, the needs of the community, your desires, and any design constraints imposed by your location. Finally, your menu must be analyzed in terms of balance and variety, taking into account the arrangement of colors, shapes, textures, and temperatures.

The kind of decisions you make at this point are crucial. Will you include seasonal specials, such as fresh salmon, or rely entirely upon frozen fish and meats? Will your breakfast menu offer only soft-boiled eggs and prunes? How many varieties of sandwiches can you make at lunch and still work the grill? Will you make your own desserts or buy them from a supplier? How good is that supplier? How reliable?

You also should plan the path of each food item as it passes through your restaurant from receiving to sale. This process will help you to spot possible bottlenecks and to decide upon design needs and equipment specifications.

Like a military strategist, you must think through the implications of all operational elements. How will the food be stored? What cooks and how many are required for preparation of each entree? Will you be able to make the quiche and the desserts in the same oven, or will you need another oven and range? Will the food be cooked to order, or held in a steam table? How will the dishwasher be able to clean the sauté pans needed for the next order when the busboy is blockading the dish area with dirty dishes?

Look at your recipes. Do you have a preponderance of soups, salads, and desserts such as tarts and pies? Who's going to make all those things? Are there enough hours in the day and enough space in your proposed kitchen for the job to be done?

The estimation of labor time is difficult, particularly if you have no experience in restaurant kitchens. Nevertheless, it is to your advantage to be thinking in terms of prep times, cooking procedures, and back-up work. Your menu items dictate everything in the kitchen. The better organized and planned the menu, the better chance you will have of designing the kitchen and scheduling the staff to accomplish your aims.

Presenting the Menu

You also should begin thinking about menu presentation: Will you use blackboards, printed menus (elegant or simple), or verbal presentation by the servers? Blackboards have the advantage of flexibility. Printed menus allow a more subtle selling approach because often they can be more attractively designed. But beware the baroque menu—the elaborate, multicolored presentation reminiscent of an art exhibition catalogue. Unless you're purchasing a year's supply of every item in the restaurant, there's a good chance you may want to change the menu shortly after you open, once you've had a little experience with the public's acceptance of the food and the restaurant's ability to cook it. Also, given the present rate of inflation, menu prices may have to be increased. If a chunk of your budget is tied up in pieces of beautiful menu paper, you're likely to hesitate about changing the numbers. Simple, printed menus work well. You cannot disguise bleak food with fancy menu graphics. Why not spend a little more on good equipment and a little less at the printer?

A personal prejudice here: I prefer straightforward menu descriptions. If you're serving Coquilles St. Jacques and want to tell me what is in the dish, I don't object. But do you need adjectives? Let the food speak for itself. "Succulent," "rich," and similar descriptive terms are more appropriate to define the quality of the dish that is actually served than to spruce up the menu descriptions. If the scallops are succulent, I will know it when they arrive at the table. If the menu has told me to expect succulence and I get scallops with the look of dried prunes, I'll figure somebody tried to trick me.

One other point about menus. Can your menu be read in the dark? I don't mean in a closet, but in your cozy, candlelit dining room. The menu that looked so great at the printer may require a flashlight to be seen without good lighting. Be particularly careful with red lettering, which is very difficult to see at night.

Similarly, consider the readability of blackboard menus. When hung on the wall, they can be difficult to see. Blackboards on movable stands won't cause your patrons eyestrain.

Portion Sizes

Another menu factor to be considered is portion size. It is important to determine exactly what amounts of each item you will serve. The size of your servings can have a tremendous impact upon profits. Based upon your personal cooking experience, it should be easy to establish portion sizes. Keep in mind that a full-course meal, from appetizer to soup to entree to dessert, can pack the average stomach quite nicely. You want to balance the size of each item with its expected place on the menu.

Once portion size and all pertinent cooking information have been established, you must write this data on recipe cards or recipe folders. You have gone through strenuous mental gymnastics to arrive at each entry, and you don't want one of your employees to exhibit too much initiative by following his own inclinations rather than your carefully worked-out recipe plans. Hence, the need to have all of this codified—ingredient amounts, cooking times and temperatures, and portion sizes.

Pricing the Menu

Once you have formulated the broad outlines of your menu, you can consider pricing each item. Be forewarned that there are more systems for menu pricing than there are methods for treating hiccups.

I intend to discuss menu pricing in general terms simply because I believe that the setting of prices can best be done in consultation with your accountant, your chef, and your other advisors. There are resources available in public and college libraries that can provide information on specific pricing methods. I recommend that you talk with your financial advisor early in the process to be sure that you are both thinking about similar methods.

Obviously, menu prices must be established before you open. Later, when you have been in operation for some time, sales records will provide useful information to help you refine your pricing.

You will not determine prices as though you were conducting business in a vacuum. If you have a good hamburger costing twelve dollars and your neighboring competitor has a good hamburger for four dollars, there is no need to wonder why yours aren't selling. Even the most rigorous approach to menu pricing cannot ignore what the competition is doing.

Now, let's take a closer look at how to price a menu. In order to decide what our menu prices should be, we must determine what "food cost" we wish to set. Food cost is the amount of money the restaurant pays for food; it is the wholesale cost, or raw cost. The ratio of food cost to sales at retail is expressed as a percentage.

The food cost can be any number, but currently it seems to be running between 33 percent and 43 percent, depending upon the type of operation, the accounting methods, and the intelligence and acumen of the owner. Restaurants specializing in Mexican or Chinese foods may run at a lower percentage because the cost of the raw ingredients is often less than for other types of restaurants.

The lower the food cost, the more money will be left from gross sales to pay other costs. However, it is unrealistic to expect the percentage to be too low, because quality definitely will suffer.

For purposes of discussion, let's elect to shoot for a 39 percent food cost. That means for every dollar we take in on sales (exclusive of sales tax), we spend $.39 for food purchases. The food-cost percentage usually is converted to a multiplying factor to be used in menu price determinations. Thus, if we want the factor for 39 percent, we divide 100 by 39, which gives us 2.564. A 33 percent food cost results in a factor of 3.03; a 50 percent cost gives a factor of 2. If the raw cost of an item, let's say an apple, is $.05, then to obtain the selling price, we multiply that cost by our factor. For our 39 percent food-cost goal, the selling price becomes $.05 × 2.6 = $.13. At 50 percent, the selling price is $.10.

The fundamental base of menu pricing is the computation of actual food costs. This is the routine that requires a pen and paper or a calculator. We must know raw costs. As an example, let's take our trusty hamburger. Reposing on the customer's plate, the hamburger is composed of a number of items:

Hamburger patty, 5 oz. @ $1.59/lb.	$.50
Bun, 1 @ $.80/dz.	.07
Fried potatoes, 4 oz. @ $.50/lb.	.13
Lettuce	.02
Tomato	.12
Pickle	.05
	$.89

(Remember that all prices used in this book are for demonstration only and have no relation to what might loosely be called the "reality" of restaurant costs.)

On the plate, the dollar value of our hamburger is $.89. Do we merely take our 39 percent food-cost factor of 2.6 and multiply it by the raw cost to give us a menu price of $2.31? As you might expect, that is too simple.

Restaurant food is more than merely the sum of its basic ingredients. We have to receive, refrigerate, and cook the food, then pay someone to serve it. There are napkins and tablecloths to consider, not to mention condiments and guest checks and natural gas and garnishes.

Therefore, some restaurateurs prefer to use a factor that will give a lower theoretical food-cost percentage. For instance, instead of using 2.6 (39 percent), they might adopt a 3 (33 percent) or even a larger factor. By that rationale, with a factor of 3, our $.89 hamburger becomes a $2.67 item.

Needless to say, we should not expect our actual food costs to be only 33 percent. There are many additional foods and condiments that are used in preparing meals, but their costs are never directly reflected in the final menu items. To cover all those foods (such as butter, salt, and fryer oil) that have costs not computed in the menu items, some operators add a flat percentage of raw costs as a contingency. Many use 10 percent. Using this number, the raw cost of our hamburger would be $.89 + (10 percent of $.89) = $.98. Multiplying by 3 gives a menu cost of $2.94.

But hamburger shrinks a little when it is cooked. Most meats do. In purchasing a hamburger, most customers understand that the restaurant begins with a given raw weight, and then a small amount is lost during cooking. However, when setting the menu price for turkey, roast beef, or another meat from which several orders may be cut, we must calculate the yield *after* the meat is cooked. We cannot very well advertise ten ounces of roast beef (based on raw weight), then serve seven ounces (the yield after trimming and cooking) and say that the stuff lost a little volume in cooking. As you can see, the whole pricing process becomes a trifle more complex. For roast beef, we might calculate the price like this:

Roast beef, as received:
100 lbs. @ $.75/lb.
Our cost $75.00

Less:
      Any usable trim for stews at the
        current price of stew meat:
        5 lbs. @ $.50/lb.   (2.50)

      Waste, such as weight of
        bones, fat, etc. @ $0.00   (0.00)

      Adjusted price $72.50

Cook and weigh meat (assume shrinkage
    after trim loss gives a weight of 85 lbs.).
    The actual price per pound is $72.50
    divided by 85.

Therefore, we use $.85/lb. to compute menu prices.

As another example, let's say we want to serve New York steak, which we want to trim out ourselves from boneless strips. The meat arrives at $3.50 per pound. We cut it into eight-ounce steaks. The raw cost of each serving is $1.75. But note, to obtain those eight ounces we must trim off fat, which composes at least 50 percent of the strip. This means the price of the steak doubles. The raw cost of an eight-ounce New York cut is $3.50.

Let's review briefly. We have said that basic pricing necessitates a determination of raw costs, including an allowance for waste and shrinkage. We then employ a factor that has been selected to give us a desired food-cost percentage. We also have noted that there are many costs not directly involved in the calculation of raw food costs but needed for the preparation and serving of food. Some consultants insist that the only accurate pricing system takes into account gas and electric charges, cooking oils, and all other hidden costs.

Other consultants believe that labor must be considered also. Before cooking, the hamburger must be pattied, the steak trimmed, the roast beef trimmed and prepped. Determining the amount of labor involved can be difficult for the uninitiated. That is why so many owners simply multiply raw food costs by a factor of three, assuming that their actual food costs will be higher and figuring that a factor of three will adequately cover labor costs as well as other expenses.

Note also that by adhering strictly to a policy of multiplying raw costs by a factor of three or four, we probably will have an unmanageably large spread between the least and most expensive menu items. The New York steak could easily become prohibitively expensive with the addition of potato, vegetable, and salad. We might want to offer it at a lower percentage markup. In expectation of higher hamburger sales, we could increase the percentage markup on that item, thereby making up in volume hamburger sales what we lost in absolute dollar profit on the steak.

Once you open, you will be basing your menu prices upon information culled from each day's business receipts. The sales mix and the frequency of sale of each menu item can alter your percentages.

When you are working your way through the menu, particularly during the recipe testing stages that involve trial-and-error studies of such factors as cooking methods, prep work, and portions, be sure to devise an accurate system for recording each food and preparation method that you test. By recording the ingredients used and the amounts, the cooking temperatures and times, the results and your comments, you will have a head start on organizing your menu.

Do not plan the menu in isolation. Test ideas and recipes on friends. Visit other restaurants. Read cookbooks. Writers such as Julia Child (*Mastering the Art of French Cooking*) and Irma Rombauer (*Joy of Cooking*) know about food. Their books can help you learn more.

Within reason, determine the parameters of your menu before your planning gets too far along. Analyzing the menu early on may save you grief later. You will know what you want to accomplish and how to achieve those goals.

While the Menu Shapes Up . . .

Although you may not as yet have a location, staff, or money, continual and concentrated thought about the entire restaurant is vital. Now that you've thought about food, have you given thought to the style of uniforms your staff will wear, the type of tablecloths and napkins, the amount of money you will need as a cash bank when you open?

Restaurants are a conglomerate of details, each of which bears on the entire operation. Tablecloths, uniforms, and cash may seem unimportant this early, but once you begin to design and construct your place, there will never seem to be enough time.

Another item that many restaurateurs unfortunately leave until the very end is the creation of a logo. Many simply do not grasp the importance of a logo; others do not understand the amount of time needed to design a logo truly representative of a restaurant.

The benefits of a well-executed logo are difficult to quantify. When my wife and I opened our bookstore in 1976, we spent many hours with Larry Green, a graphic artist and designer in San Francisco. Larry has created logos for many Northern California restaurants.

The logo he designed for Robbins Book Shop continues to intrigue people. They comment favorably upon its effectiveness and its accurate reflection of the store. A newspaper columnist has written about it, and publishers' representatives from across the country call to ask about it.

Having a pleasing logo gives you an identity that reaches far beyond the physical confines of your restaurant. The logo creates interest and provides advertising possibilities. It enhances the design of your napkins, matches, and decor. A good logo might enable you to sell just a few more dinners to people drawn by its beauty or originality. The logo is not going to be the difference between financial success and failure, but it can be a significant factor in determining the tone and style of your place.

There is an added benefit to working on your logo with a good designer: You will be forced to keep defining the goals and standards of your restaurant. Larry notes, "My experience has been best when I work with people who give information back to me. Give and take. Who know what they're trying to do. People should have a strong idea about their places, not necessarily about the logo. I should be interpreting their ideas about their place in the logo."

2

Locating and Leasing

Choosing a Location

"My advisors—my accountant, my lawyer—they all said it was a terrible location. Then I looked across at that beautiful park. I liked the view. I think if you have a good place, people will overcome obstacles to get to it."

"I'm not entirely convinced that location is so important as some people say. Before we took this place, I discovered a lot of advice from financial and supply people who said not to do it."

Those are the words of two restaurant owners who operate successfully in a large city. In cities, people are accustomed to the inconveniences of limited parking and cramped buildings. Within limits, one location in a city is often just as good or just as bad as another.

In smaller towns, however, or those with clearly defined and habitually used shopping areas, there may be a need for more careful selection of a site. Believing that your fantastic food will entice folks to drive thirty miles up a bad road may be an expensive and disastrous delusion if you live in an area where people consider a fifty-mile drive a major excursion. On the other hand, in certain regions people are more likely to drive for an hour to visit a good establishment than to suffer foul food for the convenience of staying near home.

Not everyone, even in a city, guesses correctly. Michael McCourt's place was located on 71st Street in New York. Currently a popular neighborhood, it was not so well cared for in the sixties. Michael no longer has his place, but in recalling those years he says, "I like to think I was a pioneer. I was just ahead of the times. Besides, the price was right."

In regard to decor, too, Michael's ideas were excellent if too far ahead of his contemporaries': "I wanted to do a western theme bar. In all of New York I couldn't find anything for the decor. Now look at it."

The process of finding a location can be likened to choosing a friend, spouse, new house, or good tennis racket. There are numerous possibilities, all different and all having distinct appeal and some definite disadvantages. As you begin the site-selection process, you will soon learn that most of your choices are basically unsatisfactory. After careful consideration and with an element of luck, you can narrow the choices. Be prepared to reject innumerable locations before you find one. Be patient and don't rush the process.

John Ash & Company is located in a shopping center. The owner, John Ash, does not speak highly of shopping center locations because often a restaurant is not very visible among all the other shops. In contrast, Ray Martin of Las Cruces, New Mexico, is enthusiastic about the shopping center where his restaurant, Whistleberry & Company, is located. He likes the excellent parking facilities.

There are always differing opinions. In the end, it is your

choice. It is your money and your decision. Even after deciding, you are sure to have second thoughts or that sick feeling in the tummy. No spot will be perfect.

After you have selected a community in which to locate, even if it's somewhere you have lived all your life, you must try to determine economic conditions. Again, large cities provide a different situation than small towns. Large population centers invariably offer a broader economic base (except for cities like Detroit, where one industry predominates), whereas small communities often are dependent upon specialized industries, such as agriculture, mining, or tourism. They are, therefore, more susceptible to economic fluctuations.

Armed with your skepticisms and a file folder that will gradually thicken as you acquire scraps of information, you can begin by talking to the local Chamber of Commerce and real estate agents. Other sources of information are newspaper business departments and the public relations offices of large businesses. All these people have a vested interest in presenting a bright economic picture of their town. Sift through their words and soon you will begin to get a pretty good idea of the community's economic health and its future.

If you are a stranger in town, it may be helpful to research population profiles, education levels, incomes, and social conditions. However, as in the case of most statistics, these may only confirm your own observations. Keep your eyes open as you roam the streets. The people walking there will tell you much about the community.

Eventually, you probably will have to hire a real estate agent. Robert Henn is a San Francisco attorney with extensive experience in advising restaurant owners about financing and locating. He stresses the need to shop for a real estate agent. Interview several prospective agents to evaluate their backgrounds and personalities. Then talk to people who have dealt with those agents. Ask them hard questions: Do you trust the agent? What didn't you like about the agent? Would you use the agent again?

Following the interviews and reference checks, you, the client, must decide if you like and trust the agent. Some restaurateurs prefer to go to a large firm. They retain a young, aggressive agent who has an older, experienced supervisor, the thought being that the dual attributes of energy and knowledge will be combined in the work of the two.

Bob Henn has one other suggestion regarding an agent: "Give the agent a verbal agreement that he has an exclusive, that he is the only agent you will deal with." In this arrangement, the agent knows there is a greater certainty of earning a commission because the client is dealing with a single agent.

Inevitably, your choice of locations will narrow to specific neighborhoods. The agent can give you an assessment of potential growth, new developments, problems, and assets. Talk to other business owners—not necessarily to other restaurant owners, unless your operation does not threaten theirs. Above all, talk to people who live in the town and in the area. Generally, people love to talk about restaurants. If they know you are planning one, they will readily offer an opinion. Some restaurateurs also believe that the presence of a bank in the neighborhood indicates economic stability.

Having devoted time to your menu, you can more easily accommodate your plans to the needs of the area. It is evident that a drive-in won't work too well on New York's Fifth Avenue. But will the menu you have devised fit the neighborhood you are considering? Have you priced yourself out of a particular section? Perhaps you will decide that the prices should be higher to attract a particular type of clientele.

Then, too, you should look at your competition. Most restaurateurs who do well favor a certain amount of good competition. The emphasis is upon the quality of those other operations. A neighborhood with well-run places and a reputation as a restaurant area may be favorable. If, however, people are not willing to go to a section of town because the operators seem to be competing to produce the worst food at the highest prices, then even if your place is good, it may be difficult to attract enough customers.

Having too many other restaurants around can hurt if there aren't enough customers. As Ed Moose, owner of the Washington Square Bar & Grill in San Francisco, has noted, "I think it a mad business where you can work yourself to death. There are so many variables. You can do a pretty good job and still go down."

At some point early in the site-selection process you must consult local government officials. People working in the planning, building, and fire departments are very important to you and your restaurant. From approval of architectural plans prior to opening to monthly health inspections long after your first day of operation, they will have an impact upon your business and your mental health.

You should obtain information about local codes and laws from the local authorities. Failing this sort of early education, you may well find the right location only to learn later, after much work and the expenditure of many dollars, that the city doesn't permit restaurants in that area, or that the off-street parking you have provided is inadequate, or that you do not meet health codes.

You will be awed by the number of different zoning classifications. Two adjacent parcels of land may differ in the usages permitted on them. You must be certain to understand zoning regulations. Following is a list of some of the codes you, as a restaurant operator, will be expected to follow:

Fire
Health
Use
Parking

Occupancy
Garbage
Sewage
Loading zone
Energy
Handicapped
Signage

This list is provided so that, as you begin to narrow your choices of location, you will be aware of the need to adapt to the codes. You'll find that even locations that appear suitable at first glance may cost too much to build according to the standards of the codes.

As a restaurant owner you will be required to possess several permits. Following is a broad representation of the types of permits your state and local governments may require:

Building permit
Health department permit
Fire department permit
Seller's permit (for sales tax control)
Conditional use permit

Additionally, you will need several licenses:

Fictitious name
Liquor or beer and wine (this ties into your conditional use
    permit and to Internal Revenue Service special occupa-
    tional tax regulations)
Employer's I.D. number (for tax and Social Security purposes)
Business license

Once you have selected a likely site, there are a number of additional factors to consider. One of the first, which is again influenced by your menu, relates to the specific neighborhood. The stylish restaurant with a reservations-only policy will not be as concerned about pedestrian traffic and drop-in business as a bar and grill. In its turn, the bar and grill may be less worried about the density of population in the immediate area than a breakfast place catering to office workers. If the junk-yard dog next door will frighten patrons, maybe you should not select that abandoned warehouse, even if it is cheap.

In considering a less-than-ideal location, remember that restaurants can revitalize run-down neighborhoods. It takes a clear vision to recognize potential where others have feared to go unless armed. But it has been done. If new restaurants opened only in very desirable areas, eventually there would be no room for more operators.

While we are discussing the neighborhood, you should take a look at the accessibility of your proposed site. How is the road system? Do traffic lights and street arrangement make entry and exit easy? If it is a location without easy parking, will you be able to utilize valet parking? Do you want a valet? Is the place visible to passing motorists? Will it be so hidden that finding it will require a couple of bloodhounds from the Alabama Prison System? Do you need a large sign? Will you be permitted to have a large sign?

Look at the location from another angle. Is there a scenic attraction nearby? I have had some pretty disgusting meals in sight of a beautiful ocean (in fact, the food occasionally made my stomach roll like the breakers on the beach). Do not discount aesthetic attractions. When the kids take the parents out to brunch, they often will pick the view of one place over the food of another—it gives them something to talk about.

Your real estate agent also should give you an analysis of the current market rate for space in specific areas. The agent's office will have access to information from which you can determine the rate at which commercial space is being rented. Thus you can better evaluate the rental rate you may be offered or may be willing to pay. At the same time, the agent should prepare a listing of spaces that might be suitable for your use. Be certain to shop carefully and follow all leads.

Once you find a likely space, you can give it a general examination yourself. If there is an existing building, naturally you will check the roof, walls, and floors. If you intend to take over an existing building, I strongly suggest that you spend the money to have a contractor examine the structure. If the place is so dilapidated that it obviously will have to be completely rebuilt, then you will need expert advice.

If you are looking at bare ground, you are probably already thinking about an architect. I would advise against hiring the first one you meet. In the chapter on construction, we will discuss how to select an architect. For now, be aware that before you build or remodel, you will need a professional analysis to determine if you can.

If there is an existing structure, you definitely will want to know if you qualify for the ITC (investment tax credit). According to the 1978 Tax Reform Act, it is possible to earn a tax credit on real and personal property by retaining a certain percentage of the existing structure. The ITC applies to "qualified rehabilitation property," which must be an existing building used prior to your rehabilitation. The building must be at least twenty years old. There cannot have been another ITC taken on the structure. Check with your accountant, particularly in view of tax law changes commencing in 1982.

If you are a small operator wishing to remodel an existing building, you may not absolutely need an architect. But you will need someone to draw the plans. With the drive for urban renewal and preservation of existing structures, many restaurateurs are finding it essential to work with people familiar with building codes.

Do not discount the element of luck in any aspect of your search and do not hesitate to follow any leads. Tom MacMillan and

Terry Osmonson wanted to build a restaurant in Sacramento, California. Before they found a good location, they happened to be passing through the small town of Freeport, located on the Sacramento River just a few miles from the city. There they saw an old store and gas station that seemed ideal, even though the spot had nothing in common with their original conception.

After obtaining the space, Terry and Tom were faced with a protracted struggle to secure the needed building approvals. Officials of the county and town were concerned that a restaurant would increase Freeport's traffic and noise. At last, the partners were able to have the building declared historically significant, a ruling that enabled them to proceed with construction.

The two men had no restaurant experience but did possess a clear idea of what they wanted. They hired and quickly fired an unacceptable kitchen consultant, planned their own remodeling, renovated the place, and opened. After several years, A.J. Bump's continues to be popular because it provides good food in a comfortable atmosphere.

Every aspect of a potential site must be examined: walls, roof, structural strength, foundations, bearing walls, plumbing, heating, air conditioning, and electrical wiring. This is particularly true for remodeling. I can think of no situation more loaded with potential headaches and more likely to sink a tight budget than renovation.

Bob Mulhern had more than five years experience as a bartender and waiter before taking over the lease on a neighborhood operation in San Francisco. He had hoped to upgrade the place, making it into a pleasant saloon. I talked with Bob shortly before he opened. His story may provide useful instruction.

After taking over and opening the bar, Bob began a small remodeling and upgrading project. "I hadn't gone into it in depth. I didn't know what was behind the walls." The place had been open for many years without hassles; yet when Bob began his work, he immediately encountered building code problems.

For instance, the back dining room had been rewired several years earlier, but the final inspection had never been approved. In the intervening years, the code had changed. Bob had to rewire much of that room.

"I needed more money. The gun was really to my head. The bank took weeks and weeks to approve the loan. I was out of money when they finally agreed. We went into the kitchen and found out the plumbing and electrical were shot there, too. I changed direction. We decided to make it a restaurant, not just a bar."

To those of you who haven't been in the restaurant business, this may seem a bizarre story. It isn't. Nor was that the end of Bob's difficulties. He still smiles bitterly when remembering the city clerk who closed his window precisely at his appointed quitting time. The clerk told Bob that because government workers don't get overtime, Bob would have to return the next day for his forms even though he already had been waiting most of the afternoon.

Then Bob hired an architect, a man he had known for several years: "I got a lot of talk and no plans. You hire an architect and think he's going to do things because you're paying him money.

"My stomach was shot. We lost two months because of the architect. Finally, I sat down and said, 'What do I want?' I hired a good contractor who was a friend of my brother."

On the day he fired the architect, Bob fortunately received a set of plans that enabled him to make it through city plan checks. The contractor was a blessing. So, more than six months after taking over the place, Bob had his own business. Mulhern's had no grand opening. Bob wanted to ease into the operation. He has learned the hard way, but he has, at last, achieved his goal.

The decisions are a bit easier now. "My advice to others?" comments Bob. "Don't worry about anybody else in the restaurant business. Just build your own."

The money you spend to have someone competent inspect a location may be one of your best expenditures. If you are not willing to make that nominal payment for good information, you may discover that a small project has what Ed Moose of the Washington Square Bar & Grill called "thirty years of deferred maintenance." That simple job could become more complex than the construction of the World Trade Center.

At this point in your project, it's also a good idea to make contact with neighborhood homeowner associations. If the local residents do not really care much about their area, there probably isn't such a group. But in the last few years many people have banded together to protect the character and style of their neighborhoods. It is obviously to your benefit to begin your operation by working with, not antagonizing, them.

In addition to being potential customers, neighborhood groups often have political influence in City Hall and can be helpful if you need approval of a building permit or a variance. Above all, I would not suggest trying to sneak into the neighborhood like the proverbial thief in the night. It will take you too many nights to build the place. Without your neighbors' support, you may be in the dark permanently.

Signing the Lease

Let's assume that you've found a promising location. You have met the landlord, who, all things considered, does not seem too much the ogre. He has given you a copy of the lease, suggesting it is merely a "standard restaurant lease like all the others, so you don't need to have an attorney look it over." Not true. Go directly to your lawyer.

Just as old buildings need to be carefully examined, new leases should be scrutinized by a professional. Bob Henn cautions that a tenant should *never* accept a printed form lease. It is always going to favor the landlord.

You can find entire books devoted to the intricacies of real estate deals. As a restaurateur, you probably will not have time to read much. However, you should have an attorney who knows something about restaurants, small business, and you. Don't forget—attorneys, like accountants, are advisors; they are a source of information and technical knowledge. A high percentage of them may not be well qualified to handle real estate transactions, so shop around.

You will be amazed at the number of times you must refer to your lease, even after you open. Before you sign, read the small print and check with your lawyer. The following list is not exhaustive but suggests some major points to examine in the lease.

1. *Lease term:*   Even before you find out what the place will cost, find out how many months you have. You are putting money into your restaurant; it would be nice to have enough time to recoup the investment. You probably won't get the same terms the British had in Hong Kong (ninety-nine years), but you will want three, five, or ten years with options "to renew the term." A longer term with options to renew gives you time to recoup your initial investment and to make a decent return on it.

There are locations in New York and Los Angeles where three to five years maximum is all you will be offered. Landlords in those cities never know when they will be approached by a high-rise developer. They do not want a nice, well-run restaurant to stand in the way of another office building. If you can, go for lots of time. And for renewal options.

If you are contemplating a long-term building period, it may be worthwhile to break down the lease into a "construction term" and "prime term." During construction, you will not have many customers in the place, so why should you be paying full rent, or any rent? Perhaps you can negotiate a reduction or elimination of rent while you are building. Usually the lease is worded to define construction term as extending until the restaurant opens or until a specified date, whichever comes first. After the expiration of the construction term, the prime term commences.

Also, depending upon your negotiating strength, you may be able to have the landlord ease the financial burdens of your project. Bob Henn offers some advice in this regard: "The higher stated rent a landlord can show, the greater the capitalized value of his property. If he can add another ten cents a square foot per month, that's worth far more than the actual cash income to him because a multiple gets applied to that in arriving at the value of the property. That pushes the value of his property way up.

"The tenant can give the landlord that [agree to a higher monthly rent] and get something back in return. He can get free rent up front—maybe not even just the construction period, but for a longer period of time. And he can get 'contributions to tenant improvements.'" (Those contributions are often payments made by the landlord to finance part of the tenant's construction costs.)

2. *Rent:*   Specific rent provisions may take several forms: a flat monthly rate; a percentage of gross sales; a percentage of gross sales against a fixed monthly rental.

Percentage leases are very important to shopping centers and other large or expensive projects. Generally, the tenant will pay a fixed monthly amount, then a percentage of all sales over a certain amount. For instance, your basic rent might be fixed at $1.50 per square foot. If you have 1,000 square feet, your minimum monthly rent is $1,500. Your percentage rent might be 6 percent of all sales over $25,000 per month, with the minimum monthly rent as a deduction against that overage. If you sell $25,000 or less, your rent stays at $1,500. If you sell $30,000, your rent for that month would be $1,800: You pay $1,500 minimum plus $300 (6 percent of $30,000 = $1,800, less $1,500 = $300 to pay).

The percentage rent is a risk-shifting device; the lower minimum rent you have, the less you will be affected by declining sales. Strive to negotiate a low minimum with a percentage rent that steps down as sales increase. For example, the percentage might begin at 6 percent, then, as your sales improve, go to 5.5 percent, and, with even higher sales, decline to 5 percent.

Note, too, that there are exclusions to gross sales amounts that should not necessarily be included in computing your rent base:

Employee tips
Exchange of merchandise between restaurants
Returns of merchandise to suppliers
Sales of used fixtures
The amount of city, county, state, federal sales, luxury, or
    excise taxes that are added to selling prices
Receipts from vending machines, pay telephones, valet
    parking, or employee and promotional meals sold at or below
    restaurant cost
Amounts deducted by credit card companies
Interest and dividends received by tenant

The owner of a shopping center uses the minimum rents to meet basic costs and debt service (loan repayments). From the percentage rents, the owner receives what Bob Henn calls "upside potential." That is, as tenants' sales increase, their rents will increase. And the owner also has "inflation protection," which means as everything else goes up, so do rents.

Another method that provides the landlord with inflation protection is the use of "expense pass-throughs." This term is self-explanatory. The landlord has costs associated with the building. Meeting those costs is made the tenant's responsibility. The most common pass-through is the "triple net lease," in which the tenant must pay maintenance, taxes, and insurance on the rental space.

Keep in mind that any remodeling you do—beautiful windows,

an expanded dining room—on a leased building becomes the land-lord's. Sure, you can take some of it if you move. But some of it will be classed as leasehold improvements and cannot be taken with you. If you are responsible under the lease for taxes, and the value of the space is assessed upward because of the wonderful im-provements you've made, your taxes will rise also.

Another form of pass-through occurs when the tenant is made responsible for taxes that are properly the landlord's responsibility. Be certain you understand what you must pay. While real property taxes may be passed on to you, personal property taxes should be borne only by those who own that personal property.

Infrequently, certain areas of a town may be assessed for the construction of a local community project, such as sewers. The landlord may try to make you pay the assessment. If your lease provides for assessment pass-through, the resulting tax bill could be crippling.

At some point early in the negotiating phase, you should ac-curately measure your space. This is valuable not only for compar-ison shopping among several different locations but for analyzing pass-throughs. In larger projects, many costs such as "common area maintenance" (the care of halls, elevators, and similar areas), which logically might be seen as the landlord's responsibility, are passed through to the tenants on a percentage basis. Tenant costs are determined using a ratio of individual space to total center space. As a tenant, it is important to know that the landlord is not charging you more than the appropriate percentage share.

3. *Shell*:   It is important to understand what is meant by this word in your lease. Typically, a building shell consists minimally of four walls and a roof; the floor slab is not necessarily included. Generally, the utilities are brought only to the walls ("stubbed in"). Everything else inside the shell may be the tenant's responsibility.

4. *Subletting*:   You may not like the restaurant business after you open, or things may not go as you had planned. The landlord should not have the right to "unreasonably" withhold your right to sublet, mortgage, or assign your lease.

The subletting clause also ties into lease terms and options to renew. You probably will not be earning a very large salary in your new restaurant, nor will you be making a very large percentage profit on your gross sales. A better indication of the value of your effort is "capital appreciation," which refers to the increased value, the return, you have on your investment.

To obtain the benefit of capital appreciation, you need a long lease term and a fair subletting clause. If the landlord has the option to block your assignment or sale of your lease, you may have real problems. If your business fails, you might have difficulty getting out of the lease, even if you can find a buyer for the business. Similarly, if you wish to sell a going business, the landlord might be able to impede that sale. Thus, the subletting and assignment clause directly affects your capital appreciation. Selling your restaurant for a profit, for a reasonable return on your investment, is capital appreciation. To have the landlord make that sale difficult is a costly obstacle to capital appreciation.

5. *Cost-of-living increases*:   A Consumer Price Index (C.P.I.) increase means that as inflation continues, your rent will continue to increase. The C.P.I. is a government economic indicator that charts price changes and alterations in the cost of living. Landlords often use this index as the basis for rent increases. Thus, if the C.P.I. increases by 10 percent a year, your rent may increase a like amount.

As a tenant, you should understand which government index is being used. The Bureau of the Census classifies information in two categories—"All U.S. Cities" and "Metropolitan Areas." These two are subdivided into "All Urban Consumers" and "Wage Earners."

Find out which index your lease specifies. The Department of Labor can give you a summary of the variations of each index in your region.

You also may want to discuss having a "ceiling," or "cap," put on the increases—for instance 8 percent to 10 percent. This means that no matter how high the C.P.I., your increases in rent can be no higher than your cap.

Also note the frequency of increases. Once a month is extreme; every five years is impossibly generous. Annual increases are most common. With the exception of maintenance, taxes, and insurance, leases usually do not include both a C.P.I. increase and expense pass-throughs.

6. *Contingencies*:   There are a number of items that you should consider including in your lease as contingencies. If you cannot satisfy the conditions pertaining to these details, then you should not be locked into the lease. A contingency that you cannot meet will allow you to get out of the lease.

The first contingency is a liquor license. If for any reason you cannot obtain a liquor license or a beer and wine license, then you may not want to open a restaurant in the location you've chosen, and you obviously will not need a lease on that space.

Ned Foley owns a 10,000-square-foot restaurant called Steamer Gold Landing, located in Petaluma, California. With a large bar and dining room, the restaurant employs more than seventy people. Several nights each week there is entertainment. On Friday and Saturday many people crowd into the upstairs bar. Speaking of the exuberant drinking group in his place, Ned says, "It's ironic to earn your living from a place you won't take your wife two nights of the week."

Ned's comment brings up a paradox that any restaurant owner contemplating the purchase of a liquor license should consider:

That license can be both profitable and painful. The profits from the sale of liquor are very good. However, many owners do not believe the difficulties associated with the sale of hard liquor are worth the profit.

Every state has its own laws regulating the sale and purchase of liquor licenses. Early in your project you must identify the degree of difficulty in obtaining a license. That information is part of the assessment of your business opportunity.

California is among the easiest states in which to buy a license. Other states may present more hassles. In California, a beer and wine license is available for the payment of a fee. A hard liquor license is not so readily obtainable; there is an allotment for each county. The licenses can be sold, with prices varying enormously. A San Francisco license currently runs about $25,000 to $30,000, while in Los Angeles it might cost $85,000 to $90,000. Most states are more restrictive and more expensive.

Obviously, the price of a liquor license will alter your concept of your restaurant. It will increase your expenses and influence your design. And don't forget that liquor liability laws make a restaurant and its staff responsible should a drinker injure or kill someone after leaving that establishment. These laws apply in many states. Insurance to cover liquor liability can be prohibitively expensive.

The second contingency to include is that you must be able to get all other necessary government approvals, licenses, permits, and variances.

Third, if your financing is not in place at the time you're signing the lease, specify that should you not be able to obtain the money, the lease is not binding. It is hard to build without money.

As a final contingency, specify that you be allowed to inspect the site to verify its conformation with the lease description.

Beyond these points, there are many others to be examined. Check on maintenance: Who is responsible for repairs inside and outside the space? Be certain the lease language is clear, as attorneys are not always careful about the wording in leases.

The lease on a large space can run to scores of pages. A competent attorney's assistance may save you much grief. Be absolutely certain that everything is clear and all questions resolved before you sign.

3

Capital Costs

In order to build your dream restaurant you need money. If you have unlimited funds and no wish to conserve money, you will not need to plan your capital budget very carefully. If, however, you anticipate making a bid for financial aid from a banker, an investment partnership, or even Uncle Harry, who's been working the tables in Las Vegas, you will have to demonstrate what your operation will cost to build, what it might make (if anything), and what expenses you expect to encounter.

These compilations of numbers are called pro formas, estimates, or projections. Although they are all guesses, it is possible to refine them. With the inclusion of a fudge factor—a "contingency factor," to use the jargon—you actually may come relatively close to predicting what your real costs will be.

As in the case of menu planning, this sort of work requires thinking. If you are not comfortable with numbers, it can be likened to the pain of preparing an income tax return. But it pays off. You will be forced to decide which aspects of the restaurant are vital, because you will have examined them all in terms of menu and

45

finances. And because every square inch of the restaurant and every piece of equipment or decor is costing money, this budgeting will allow you to test your decisions.

The Construction Budget

Remember, as you go through this section, that the banker is not particularly interested in your plan to build the finest restaurant in twenty states. The banker wants to know if you will repay the loan. Take some time to work out the numbers. If possible, talk over your plans with someone. Articulating ideas does wonders for separating decent thoughts from vague, imaginative flights.

The process also will reduce, if not necessarily prevent, expensive surprises—those disturbing flashes that snap you wide awake in the middle of the night. But before you grab the calculator, jump in your car and motor down to your local restaurant supply house. I realize that in some areas of the country that may not be so easy. At least make an effort to view equipment and to obtain equipment catalogues and price lists.

Restaurant supply firms can be extremely useful. After you are open, they will sell you virtually all the supplies you need. These firms are also a convenient source of reconditioned, used equipment; so investigate this section of the business before spending for the shiny new models.

Restaurant auctions are another source of equipment. As in the case of all auctions, caution is required. Before bidding on another restaurant's castoffs, be sure you know what a new item would cost and what condition the old one is in. Too many people get caught up in the bidding fever and pay too much for grease-encrusted junk.

What many people do not know is that restaurant supply

houses often have a restaurant design capability. Most are especially adept at kitchen design. Several can create entire restaurants. I am not saying that you must use these services, but be aware that they exist. When choosing such a service, be as selective as you would be in hiring an architect.

Ross Button is a sales representative for Royal Supply in San Francisco. He has been in the food-service business for seventeen years. During that time he has witnessed the birth pangs of many restaurants. Needless to say, he has acquired a few opinions about new operations. In discussing the design and service functions of his supply company, Ross says, "I'm a part-time employee for whoever buys from me. If they come to us before opening, we can draw up an agreement to design the kitchen. If the restaurant follows the design, there's no charge for the drawings. If not, there's a fee for the time. Right now it's running about thirty dollars an hour."

Before you get too excited about utilizing those design services, remember that any equipment specifications included in the design will be for equipment that firm sells. That's how they pay for the design services. If you need and like a company's line of products, there's no problem. But shop around.

Back home, you already have your tentative menu priced out; so it's time to fit the menu to a hypothetical restaurant. To illustrate the budgeting process, I have created two fictitious restaurants: Chez Petite and Chez Grande. We will examine their start-up costs and, for the smaller, estimate its sales and expenses. After reading through the sample expenditure lists, you should have a better idea of the type of costs you will encounter. Again, the lists are not meant to be exhaustive but suggestive of areas you need to think about.

Each of our hypothetical restaurants will have different needs and different problems to solve. In both cases, the situation is that we already have a certain amount of money and will have to raise the rest of our capital from outside sources. Therefore, it is necessary to know roughly how much we will need.

For Chez Petite, we are looking into the possibility of creating a small restaurant in an existing building that presently houses an antique store. The shell of the building is fine, the façade inviting. The walls, ceiling, and floor are in good condition. Only the interior space of approximately 1,500 square feet must be converted to our restaurant usage. We believe we will begin with only forty-nine seats for dining. That will give our staff and us a chance to organize the operation. Occupancy of forty-nine also keeps us under the code limit for "public assembly." To seat more than forty-nine requires adherence to building and occupancy standards that are more detailed and would substantially increase our construction costs.

Across the street, we have excellent ideas for developing Chez Grande but not much cash. We therefore assume the role of general partner in an investment partnership that will buy the bare ground and build an 8,000-square-foot restaurant seating approximately two hundred and having a full bar.

The menus for our two restaurants differ accordingly. Chez Petite will offer two or three appetizers and two entree selections each evening. For lunch, soups and limited specials such as quiche will be served. Initially, desserts will be purchased from suppliers.

Chez Grande will offer more than half a dozen appetizers, a dozen entrees for both lunch and dinner, eight desserts, assorted specials, and numerous side dishes.

We already have selected the kitchen equipment (see Chapter Five, "Kitchen Design"). For both places we first must determine what work is necessary on the walls, floors, and roof to enclose the space. Chez Grande will require complex bidding and building, so our first task is find an architect, then a contractor.

Chez Petite is much simpler. Since the shell is in good condition, we need only worry about covering the kitchen walls with material that meets the code specifications of the county health department. Our next step is to make a cost estimate of major kitchen equipment and work:

Stove	$ 1,500
Toaster	150
Cheese melter	500
Reach-in refrigerator	600
Food processor	250
Garbage disposal	500
Ice machine (lease deposit)	500
Dishwashing machine (lease deposit)	500
Prep table	500
Hood over cooking line (including fire system)	7,000
Make-up air system	1,500
Sinks and tray slides at dishwashing ares ($125/linear foot)	1,200
Cover part of kitchen wall to a height of six feet with Marlite ($6/square foot)	900
Magnasite floor ($12/square foot)	3,600
Stainless steel on walls behind cooking line	1,000
Shelves for storeroom	250
Additional fire extinguishers	100
Paint for kitchen (our labor)	100
Labor to install and hook up cooking equipment	500
Total	$21,150

Some of you may look at these kitchen costs skeptically; you may say that your entire restaurant could be built for this amount. That may be true. I am attempting to give as complete a picture as possible of most of the known costs. With initiative and friends, with a little horse trading and mechanical know-how, many of these costs can be substantially reduced. But don't assume that because a supplier or subcontractor says it can be done cheaper, it can—or will be.

At Chez Petite, we are electing to lease the dishwashing machine and the ice machine. It is possible to lease virtually everything, from all the equipment to a new floor. You also may find that the equipment supply houses are willing to help finance your purchases for a short term. Both these methods will reduce your initial investment costs.

Chez Grande, being grander and bigger, will require more of everything. Naturally, we have had to buy the land and construct the entire building. Before looking at new construction costs, let's examine our kitchen needs.

We know we will have two or three stoves, two grills, a broiler, two or three fryers, long pass shelves with several food warmers, a steam table, a walk-in refrigerator with integral walk-in freezer, milk dispensers, kitchen duck boards, a food mixer, etc. Major equipment at Chez Grande will cost in the neighborhood of $100,000.

We know that in Chez Petite only the dining room walls need paint. Beyond that, we'll change the lighting slightly, install tables and chairs, and, because it is located in a trendy part of town, an espresso machine. We will rent the table linen from a linen supply company. Here, then, are the estimated costs for the public spaces at Chez Petite:

Cash register	$1,000
Espresso machine	2,500
Coffee grinder	200
Tables, 15 @ $100	1,500
Chairs, 55 @ $50	2,750

One food-service station (Grandma's old sideboard)	250
Dining room paint (our labor)	200
Two public restrooms (including fixtures for the handicapped, paint, plumbing, electrical)	10,000
Total	$18,400

Notice that we lucked out. Think of the added expense to install or remodel walls (including framing and sheet rock, complete electrical, and carpet). We haven't included wall decor because Grandma has several old photos she'll let us use for a small fee.

Chez Grande needs more of everything—more chairs, more tables, five or six specially made food-server stations, and more menus. And since there will be a complete bar, we need to buy duckboards, bar stools, a glass washer, blenders, reach-in refrigeration, sinks, glassware, pour spouts, fruit containers, etc.

We have not begun construction on Chez Grande because the architect is still working on the plans. The first estimate is that the basic building will cost approximately $800,000 for 8,000 square feet. That price does not account for fixtures, only construction of the shell. Here is a very small part of what that money will purchase:

Permits	Floor covering
Construction office	Sheet metal
Phone	Lighting
Grading	Heating, ventilation, and air conditioning
Framing	
Roofing	Mill work—server stations, bar, etc.
Doors and hardware	
Exhaust hood	Plumbing
Electrical	

Until recently, Les Horton was a building contractor; currently he is a construction supervisor and an estimator. Over the years, Les has built many restaurants. He believes that in California it now costs at least $100 per square foot to build a new restaurant. To remodel an existing structure costs $50 to $85 per square foot, depending upon the work involved. Nationwide, the average cost for new construction is approximately $80 to $90 per square foot and $35 to $80 per square foot for remodeling.

Let's return to Chez Petite, where we continue to press the add button on our calculator. We have listed the major expenses in the kitchen and dining room. Fortunately, we did not have to remodel. Expenditures thus far total $39,550.

But are these all the expenses? Even though the major budget items are accounted for, we cannot cook without pots and pans. Here, then, is a listing of assorted small equipment we must buy:

Portion scale	$ 60
Mop	12
Mop bucket	32
Garbage cans, 4 @ $15	60
Egg pans (assorted)	75
Sauce pans (assorted)	75
Mixing bowls	85
Ladles	30
Frying-pan covers	50
Whips	20
Knives (assorted)	100

We will need many more small kitchen items. The number depends upon our menu and cooking techniques. For Chez Petite, we will allot a total of $1,000 for this equipment.

We also need something on which to serve the food, so we will order crockery. The traditional amount of crockery to have on hand is two-and-a-half to three times the total number of seats. If we have 49 seats, we need about 150 plates with comparable amounts of other pieces. The thinking behind this method is that we will have one complete set in the dining room, one set being washed, and one back-up set.

Ross Button has known several operators who tried to open with the wrong crockery: "The biggest sin that new owners make is not buying their chinaware on time. If all you want to use is what the supplier stocks, then there won't be much of a problem. Choose a special pattern or break some before opening, and you're looking at 120 days lead time. If it isn't standard, be careful."

Perhaps you won't need three times your seating capacity in place settings. But be sure you understand that it takes a lot of crockery to run a small restaurant. For Chez Petite, we will order conservatively and budget another $1,500 for such items as:

Wine glasses
Crockery
    Large plates
    Salad plates
    Cups
    Saucers
    Soup bowls
    Plates (liners) for soup bowls
    Creamers
    Teapots
Silverware (flatware)
    Knives
    Forks
    Spoons
    Soup spoons
Ashtrays
Salt and pepper shakers
Candleholders for tables
Matches
Water pitchers
Ice bucket
Silverware tray

As for coffee equipment, the company from whom you buy your coffee may or may not supply the coffee machine, pots, and warmers free of charge. Don't count on it just because your restaurant will be serving their coffee.

In comparison, Chez Grande will need about $10,000 for small kitchen equipment and another $10,000 for crockery and related dining room needs. The kitchen designer, working with the architect, already has estimated major kitchen equipment at $100,000 and other fixtures at $45,000. In all these computations for Chez Grande, keep in mind that the cost of the bare ground has not been included.

Chez Petite's budget is coming along well. At $42,050, it seems cheap. But we are not finished. Some of the subcontractors are just now submitting their bids:

Plumbing (all gas lines, sprinkler system, kitchen-floor drains, waste lines, sinks, etc.)	$ 7,600
Electrical (kitchen and dining room outlets, additional lighting fixtures)	700
Architectural drawings	1,000
Beer and wine license (California)	400
Opening inventories	
Food	800
Beer and wines	700
Legal and accounting fees	2,000
Pre-opening advertising and promotion	1,000
Total	$14,200

Our budget is now at $56,250. Here, we can apply our contingency factor. Since we have been fairly conservative and conscientious, and since we have faith in our projections, we will use an 8 percent contingency. This covers costs we may have forgotten to include, as well as unexpected price increases. Therefore, 8 percent of $56,250 = $4,500. The construction budget is now determined by adding the contingency amount to the basic costs: $56,250 + $4,500 = $60,750.

Not bad. But look again. What might we have forgotten? The security deposit to the landlord for first and last month's rent and purchase of the existing lease for the retail business currently operating in the space—these two items alone could easily add $10,000.

Let's say that we need $1,500 to buy the antique store's lease. The security deposit is $3,000 (roughly equivalent to two months of rent). If we are in a hot climate, we may need air conditioning, which could add another $10,000 to our costs. And how about funding for training the staff and for the pre-opening dinners that are vital to our preparation?

Perhaps we don't really need air conditioning (we will leave the doors open and talk more during hot weather to circulate the air). We guess that we will need at least three trial dinners to spot rough areas of preparation and service. This will take another $1,000.

Normally, we cannot expect to be making money during the first weeks of operation. We should include an amount to cover "operational loss before stabilization." This figure tells us how much more money will be needed in those early weeks to meet continuing expenses before we sell enough food to cover all costs. The period could be a month, maybe six months. If our budget is stretched already, those early weeks could break us. Let's give ourselves another $6,000 to cover the rocky periods. We don't have to spend it if business is better than expected.

Now let's add those numbers to our basic construction budget, excluding our first contingency number. Be sitting down when you press the "total" button.

Original estimate	$56,250
Plus	
Lease purchase from existing tenant	1,500

Security deposit	3,000
Pre-opening dinners	1,000
Loss before stabilization	6,000
Total	67,750
Plus 8 percent contingency	5,420
TOTAL FOR CHEZ PETITE	**$73,170**

Before you rush off to buy into that money-market fund your friend told you about, don't forget that this is an estimate. Remember, too, that we did not have to do anything substantial to the shell to meet code requirements. If we had, that would have significantly increased costs.

On the other hand, it is certainly possible to open a small restaurant for less money, but you have to be quick on your feet and good with your hands. Using Les Horton's estimates for remodeling costs, we easily could have invested thousands more to rebuild the place. A small restaurant could be built for less than $40,000, but it depends on what you have and what you can use and what you can make do with. My aim is to try to familiarize you with all the details you will be obliged to consider.

If Chez Petite's costs look enormous, take a peek at Chez Grande, where the expenses are mounting like Defense Department cost overruns. You will recall that we left them with a token initial investment of considerable proportions:

Building construction	$800,000
(excluding site acquisition)	
Kitchen	100,000
Fixtures and equipment	45,000
Small kitchen equipment	10,000
Crockery and related equipment	10,000
Total	$965,000

That leaves very little change from the first million. What follows is a sampling of Chez Grande's additional costs, which are similar to Chez Petite's but proportionally higher:

Architecture	$ 60,000
Construction supervision	50,000
Construction insurance	3,000
Liquor license (California)	40,000
Opening inventory	
Food	15,000
Liquor and wines	30,000
Legal and accounting fees	30,000
Advertising and promotion	8,000
Telephone	1,000
Total	$237,000

Because this is a big project and we have not included such costs as staff training (this place eventually may have a staff of seventy-five, so you can be sure that it will cost quite a bit to train everyone), landscaping, etc. and etc., we will add a 10 percent contingency:

Construction costs	$1,202,000
10 percent contingency	120,200
Total	$1,322,200

Let's stop here.

My intention has not been to list every expense, just most of them. In many types of small business, the owner installs shelves, lights, carpets, and a few miscellaneous pieces of equipment and then opens. Restaurants are usually not so easy.

Obviously, our two restaurant examples are meant to illustrate basic costs. Chez Petite could be built for less. Chez Grande undoubtedly will cost more than a million and a half, but then the expected profits are large also. Otherwise, those steely-eyed investors wouldn't be donating their money to the effort.

Unless you've been taking your vitamins, I guess you're probably tired of running around town getting catalogues and price estimates. At least you now have a good feel for what your new restaurant is going to cost.

Projecting Income and Expenses

The next stage of the design involves another stint at your desk. Since you're not building this place for practice, you want to have an idea of your costs and profit. This involves analyzing income and expenses.

Here again, this exercise is beneficial because you will have to think through another aspect of your operation. The process also provides information your banker will want. Your estimates of income and expenses will be helpful when you draw up your pro formas for your loan proposals.

First, you must determine how well and how poorly your restaurant might do. From the menu prices you already have computed, you should be able to guess at the approximate average guest check. In addition, you will need more information:

>Guest check average, per person, for each meal period
>Number of restaurant seats
>Number of operating days
>Number of hours open each day
>Turns—the number of bodies you expect to feed
>>based upon the number of seats. If Chez Petite
>>has 49 seats and feeds 75 people at dinner,
>>the restaurant has 1½ turns.

It is easy to list these requirements, but not so easy to figure them out. Here is a sample for Chez Petite, which is located in a small town:

Assumptions

Seats	49

Operating days and hours
  Lunch—six days each week
    11:00 A.M. to 3:00 P.M.—4 hours
    (Closed Sunday)
  Dinner—four nights each week
    5:30 P.M. to 11:00 P.M.—5½ hours
    (Closed Sunday, Monday, Tuesday)

Average guest check per customer

Lunch	
Beverage	**$1.50**
Food	4.25
Lunch average	**$5.75**
Dinner	
Beverage	**$3.00**
Food	8.50
Dessert and coffee	1.25
Dinner average	**$12.75**

Turns	
Lunch—1¾	85 customers
Dinner—1½	75 customers

Daily sales (excluding sales tax)	
Lunch (85 × $5.75)	$488.75
Dinner (75 × $12.75)	956.25
Total daily sales	$1,445.00

Yearly sales	
Lunch (6 days × 50 weeks)	$146,625.00
Dinner (4 nights × 50 weeks)	191,250.00
Total annual sales	$337,875.00

The figure for total annual sales looks promising, but now we must calculate expenses. For Chez Petite, we will assume that one of us (an owner) is the hard-working chef and will do most of the cooking. If we had to hire a chef because the owner was working the dining room, our labor expenses would increase dramatically. Basically, we will require the following employees:

Food servers—two each shift
Busboy (or girl)—one each shift
Dishwasher—one each shift
Additional cook—one each shift

To calculate labor costs, you will have to know the local pay scale and make broad assumptions about how you intend to schedule and pay your staff. Here, too, you will appreciate the thought you have put into the menu. It determines the style of service and the number of people needed to perform that service and to prepare the food.

For Chez Petite, with its good, basic food, we assume that one server can competently handle six or seven tables of four people. More elaborate service would necessarily reduce that number. To assign more than seven tables to each server invites chaos. Hence, in the dining room at Chez Petite we will have two servers, with one having fewer tables but also acting as host, telephone answerer, and general public-relations type.

The busboy (girl, person, woman, man) is vital. The work involves quickly clearing and setting tables, as well as running food from kitchen to tables. The busboy does much to keep the food servers from panicking.

During slack periods, the dishwasher can perform cleaning duties and help with the prep work. Based upon our menu, we have decided that a prep cook is required for each shift. As the place becomes more popular, and the owner more tired, we may have to add another part-time cook.

Following is a rough approximation of salaries:

Food servers
$3.50 per hour, slightly above current
minimum wage

The servers and busboy must come to work
an hour before opening to set up the dining
room and perform side work, such as filling
salt shakers or dusting ledges. They also
have cleaning duties after closing.

Lunch—$3.50 × 2 servers × 5.5 hours	
Daily lunch salaries	$38.50
Dinner—$3.50 × 2 servers × 7 hours	
Daily dinner salaries	$49.00
Yearly salaries	
$38.50 × 6 days × 50 weeks	$11,550.00
$49.00 × 4 nights × 50 weeks	9,800.00
Annual food-server salaries	$21,350.00

Buspeople
$3.50 per hour (Don't forget
that food servers and buspeople
also receive tips.)

Lunch—$3.50 ×1 busperson × 5.5 hours	
Daily lunch salaries	$19.25
Dinner—$3.50 × 1 busperson × 7 hours	
Daily dinner salaries	$24.50
Yearly salaries	
$19.25 × 6 days × 50 weeks	$ 5,775.00
$24.50 × 4 nights × 50 weeks	4,900.00
Annual busing salaries	$10,675.00

Dishwasher
$4.50 per hour (This job is traditionally
an unattractive drudgery. Because we want
good workers and because the dishwasher, if good,
will advance to another position, we will pay
a little more than minimum wage. It is still
not a princely sum.)

Lunch and dinner shifts are 8 hours × $4.50 × 1 dishwasher	$36.00

Yearly salaries

$36.00 × 6 days × 50 weeks	$10,800.00
$36.00 × 4 nights × 50 weeks	7,200.00
Annual dishwashing salaries	$18,000.00

Prep cook
$6.00 per hour

Lunch and dinner shifts are 8 hours × $6.00 × 1 cook	$48.00

Yearly salaries

$48.00 × 6 days × 50 weeks	$14,400.00
$48.00 × 4 nights × 50 weeks	9,600.00
Annual prep-cook salaries	$24,000.00

Our annual salaries will total about $74,025, or approximately 21.9 percent of our gross sales. That is an excellent labor percentage. But note that it does not include such expenditures as compensation insurance and payroll taxes. The salaries could easily be higher if Chez Petite is busier than expected and if we need more workers.

We will assume that our food supplies will total about 39 percent of our gross sales. Again, not a bad number. In expensive regions, you may even run in the low forties for food costs. At Chez Petite, we will spend $131,771 for food this year ($337,875 × 39 percent = $131,771).

The basic costs for buying, cooking, and serving the food are 39 percent plus 21.9 percent times our gross sales, or about $205,765.

We also have several expenses related to keeping the place open. These "direct expenses" will vary. All are, to a degree, controllable. The percentage of gross sales that each expense represents is variable. The following should not be taken as the only possible expenses or percentages:

Advertising	.6	percent of gross sales
Cleaning and maintenance	1.4	
Laundry	1.5	
Equipment maintenance	.2	
Promotion	.4	
Repairs	.4	
Restaurant supplies	1.0	
Serviceware	1.0	
Miscellaneous	1.0	
Total direct expenses	7.5	percent

For Chez Petite, 7.5 percent of $337,875 is $25,340.

We also have "administrative expenses," which are more stable than direct expenses and not always susceptible to control:

Payroll taxes and insurance	1.4	percent of gross sales
Credit card costs	1.3	
Depreciation	3.0	
Dues and subscriptions	.1	
Insurance	1.0	
Professional services	1.0	
Rent	7.0	
Taxes and licenses	.6	
Telephone	.4	
Utilities	1.3	
Miscellaneous	1.0	
Total administrative expenses	18.1	percent

At our restaurant, 18.1 percent of $337,875 is $61,115. Note that if our rent were 6.5 percent of gross sales instead of 7.0 percent—a difference of only .5 percent—our administrative expenses would be $59,466. More important, we would have an additional $1,649 at the end of the year. Don't sneer at those percentage points.

The summary of our projections for Chez Petite is:

Gross sales	$337,875
Purchases	(131,771)
Labor (does not include payroll	
taxes and insurance)	(74,025)
Direct expenses	(25,340)
Administrative expenses	(61,115)
Total operating profit	$45,624

Not bad—a 13.5 percent profit our first try. But wait. We have not included a repayment of principal and interest on the loan from our banker or investment group. Nor have we deducted federal and state income taxes. And of significance to ourselves, we have given the owner nothing.

We will have to recompute our projections. Virtually every number in these lists is subject to manipulation. Remember the impact of a .5 percent rent difference on yearly profit? For your restaurant, perhaps you will decide that your gross sales will be higher because you will alter menu prices or have more customers. Maybe you can reduce the cost of goods or a few of the direct expenses.

Move the numbers around, but do not attempt too many changes at once. And keep things realistic. The purpose of this exercise is to give you a worst probable case, a best probable case, and a most probable. Your estimates must seem possible, not improbable.

For Chez Grande, we would have to calculate similar cost estimates. Because it's a larger operation, with more people, more suppliers, and more of everything, the projections are necessarily more complex, but the basis is the same. Move the numbers around logically until you obtain a clear idea of what may happen to your restaurant's financial situation. The exercise makes you think. It also demonstrates to others with money to lend that you have done your homework and know roughly what to expect.

The determination of capital costs is a slog, an often tedious and time-consuming struggle. Like death and taxes, it is impossible to avoid. On the other hand, the benefits are more immediate and more tangible than those derived from taxes.

4

Financing

A contented restaurateur in Sacramento, California, maintains that one of the best aspects of having a good restaurant is doing the job well, the "pride of ownership." Carl Packard, a commercial developer, responds to that statement: "I don't believe that banks consider pride of ownership as a form of capital."

Both men are correct. For you, the owner who dreams of building an excellent, productive establishment, the pride associated with ownership is a definite benefit. You are interested in cooking and decor, in providing quality products for your customers and a pleasant working environment for your staff, in earning a reasonable profit, and in the intangible rewards of recognition from your friends and associates. The people you ask to fund the restaurant are interested in your knowledge of intelligent, profitable operations and your ability to repay the loan.

Sue Weymouth is the branch manager for a major California bank in the Cow Hollow neighborhood of San Francisco. During her years in the area, she has seen many new restaurants open and almost as many fail. Although her policy and the policy of her bank in regard to restaurant loans is not absolute opposition, she says the odds of getting a loan for a new restaurant are not favorable.

Sue describes some of the problems she has noted: "We are very negative about restaurant loans because the chances of failure are very high. Most people think they're going to make a killing in the business. They fail because they haven't done enough research, they have no management ability, and they haven't the capability to run a restaurant. And they have no reserve capital."

She gestures to a large restaurant visible from the bank's window: "It's a perfect example. The owner had lots of money, but he put everything into the place and had no reserve." The restaurant purportedly cost more than a million dollars to build. It folded in six months.

Why bother? Don't waste time applying for a bank loan unless you are able to demonstrate an ability to meet their standards of fiscal strength, managerial ability, and restaurant knowledge. Try Uncle Harry or the casino tables. You will have more fun, and the odds may be slightly better.

There undoubtedly are as many sources of restaurant funding as types of restaurants. In this chapter we will touch briefly upon a few aspects of financing. There are professionals in the field who can provide you with detailed information, as well as books that examine business financing in more depth.

Very little about restaurant financing is different from that associated with other small businesses. The risk is merely greater. Perhaps an appreciation of the pitfalls will lessen the chances for error.

Remember that you will never get a loan for a longer period of time than your lease term. This is another good argument for a long-term lease. Also, for those of you who own the site and wish to use it as collateral, remember that the value of real estate is not always what you would like it to be. Generally, the building and your improvements cannot be used for anything other than a restaurant. If you default, a banker stuck with the property must find another operator. Therefore, you may find that bankers discount the value of the real estate to the value of the raw land or to the value of the raw land plus the building shell.

Bob Henn advocates using other people's money to finance restaurants. He cautions that getting this capital is competitive. There always is a demand for money, so you must be prepared to pay to use what is available. Additionally, the entire process is highly regulated and very complex. Money is harder to get than you think. This last point is confirmed in discussion with restaurateurs throughout the nation who cite the difficulties of obtaining financing as the least pleasurable aspect of their projects.

Essentially, you will find there are two broad methods of funding your dream—debt financing and equity financing. In debt financing, we are talking about your debt, not someone else's. You are advanced a fixed sum in exchange for a promise to repay both the principal and the interest charges assessed for the privilege of using the money. To guarantee your repayment, you must provide collateral, which the lender will own should you default on the payment. Collateral may include, but is not restricted to, the restaurant shell, the furnishings and fixtures, stocks, your house, other real estate holdings, and other assets.

Broadly stated, equity financing assumes that the lender is financing part of your operation in exchange for a share of the profits (if and when you have profits) and for other financial advantages, such as the chance for sheltering taxes. In essence, the equity lender owns a portion of the restaurant. The borrower must share the fruits of his labors with the lender. Usually the equity investor is repaid with a combination of tax-sheltering advantages and a percentage of the profits or of the gross sales.

Although you undoubtedly can arrange and structure debt financing yourself, equity financing can be very complex. It usually requires professional advice because taxes, methods of reimbursement, and other detailed factors are involved.

Banks are a source of debt financing. Friends and relatives

may provide debt or equity financing. Investors and investor partnerships are usually intent upon equity financing.

Most people understand that interest charges are a means whereby lenders are paid for the use of money. This method of payment also is used when Mom and Dad or friends are willing to loan you start-up capital. Bob Henn refers to parental money as "receiving your inheritance early."

At the local stationery store you will find simple promissory note forms that can be used for making financial arrangements with these generous souls. You need only establish the terms of repayment and the probable course of action should the restaurant fail. Generally, the interest will run on the principal, but repayment will be deferred for a time to give the restaurant a chance to stabilize. Loans of this type offer no tax advantages to the lender.

Be careful, however, for money problems can quickly destroy years of friendship and respect. Many friends, anxious to help you, may advance funds but not truly be in a position to absorb losses, or suddenly may need the money themselves. Because of their trust, you should be particularly careful with relatives in assessing your chances of success and in accepting money from them.

Banks and, by extension, the Small Business Administration, are a major source of financing. Commercial loans are usually for a relatively short term (say, three to five years), and they have interest rates based upon various factors, such as the prime rate, your credit worthiness, and, it seems on occasion, the phase of the moon. Banks generally require that the borrower contribute at least 50 percent of the financing. The borrower's money cannot be based upon another loan.

The Small Business Administration is a secondary source of funds through SBA loans with participating banks or SBA direct loans. If you are turned down for a loan by at least two commercial lenders, you may be eligible for a guaranteed loan through the SBA. The loan package is tedious to complete but, if you want the money, it may be worthwhile.

The terms of the loan are generally less rigorous than regular commercial deals since the SBA, a government agency, is guaranteeing up to 90 percent of the loan. Banks usually have the required information and loan officers to facilitate the application.

Direct loans from the SBA are another possibility. Again, the requirements differ, as do the benefits; so direct your inquiries to your local SBA office. There are minority and regional programs for which you may be eligible.

When applying for a commercial loan, remember that you are competing for money. It is to your benefit to prepare an attractive, accurate loan proposal. Just as you would not hire a chef without checking references and experience, the bank is not going to lend you money because you are cute and dress well.

Although bankers have an unfair reputation as being cynical and hard as prison guards, they are usually just careful and conservative. When a flamboyant restaurant visionary bursts upon them like the proverbial fox among chickens, they naturally tend to become quite busy with other work. Your job is to convince them that you can open and operate a profitable restaurant.

You may succeed in deluding them by judiciously altering a few negatives to positives, but what good will the loan do you if you fail anyway? You will have lost your investment and still be on the hook for the bank loan. Have the courage to knock your ego over the head. If, after pushing your numbers around, you discover that you will be out of money a week after you open, don't try fabricating numbers so that your projections look good. You cannot eat the loan coupons nor drink the red ink on the past-due invoices.

Spend time on your loan application. Analyze and understand it. Arrange it intelligently. Your proposal should include a statement of your purposes, what you intend to do with the money, where your restaurant will fit into the market, and why, based upon market research, there is a need for your place. Tell the banker what other restaurateurs are doing and why they fail to provide the type of services you envision. Describe your promotional plans and the advantages of the location. Mention pertinent lease terms. If you already have a lease in hand, give your banker a copy.

Remember those capital-cost projections we discussed in the last chapter? The banker will want to see those to determine how you will be spending the money. You also need a projected income and cash flow statement for at least the first year of operation, perhaps longer. Your banker may want an analysis of your break-even point. You will have to supply a personal financial statement, as will anyone involved in funding or managing the restaurant. Be prepared to guarantee the loan personally, even if the restaurant is to be operated as a corporation.

Here again, one of the benefits of doing this work is that you will be examining your ideas and thinking constructively. After preparing this proposal for your banker, you should be familiar with every financial aspect of your project.

Sue Weymouth admonishes prospective borrowers to remember that income from their place during the first few years undoubtedly will be slim or nonexistent. That is the reason commercial lenders often demand an adequate income stream not related to the restaurant. If you cannot make your house payments or even cover the inevitable restaurant operating deficits of the early months, the bank naturally will wonder how the loan will be repaid.

Many operators are quite capable of accurately predicting expenses. But their estimates of sales and income often have no more factual basis or accuracy than the fantasies of a child. Inexperienced restaurateurs often grossly exaggerate their estimated success, a condition not limited to restaurants, as witness the accuracy of government budget planners. But bankers recognize this failing and guard against it. That is one reason they like experienced operators who generally have less grandiose expectations.

Sue also cautions those of you considering the purchase of an existing place: "Very frequently you cannot get accurate figures on sales from prior owners. They are reluctant to release sales figures, many times because they may have been taking cash on the side (taking money and not reporting sales) and don't want that fact revealed."

It is relatively simple to understand why bankers would loan money in expectation of being paid for the use of the money without their having to work to earn the payment. But why would anyone want to be an equity lender and participate in the risk of a restaurant?

Of course, there's the glamor, undoubtedly one of the factors that attracted you to the business. Or call it ego. Bob Henn acknowledges the idea of ego involvement but stresses what he casually calls "upside potential." That means the investor believes that there is a potential for making a high return on the investment. After analyzing your proposal, the investor assumes your restaurant has the chance to make money and believes that the benefits are worth the risk.

Investors receive not only a share of possible profits, but immediate tax advantages as well. It is the dual benefits—tax advantages and the allure of success—that are attractive. Instead of a guaranteed return in the form of interest payments or from investments in treasury certificates or money funds, you offer the investor glamor and excitement coupled with immediate tax benefits and future possibilities.

As an individual making large capital investments, you are entitled to various tax considerations. These tax incentives offset, to a certain extent, your massive expenditures. They include such categories as depreciation and investment tax credit (ITC).

Typically, most new restaurant owners have no need for tax benefits, since they have little income to be taxed. They do have need for investment money. On the other hand, investors usually have plenty of income and need tax sheltering. The operator has the shelters to exchange for their money.

Ordinarily—I say again, ordinarily—for lenders to get tax advantages they must be equity investors. The term "pass through" indicates the manner in which tax shelters such as depreciation are made available to an investor.

Establishing investor partnerships is complex and requires assistance from experts to structure properly. There are ways to provide 100 percent of the tax shelter to your investors. But tax sheltering is only part of the deal. There must be that promise of future gain. Bob Henn points out that, "Any sensible accountant and any sensible lawyer will tell you that you don't ever make an investment because of the tax shelter. You make it because it's good economically. The tax shelter is your sweetener; it may push it over the top. Don't fool yourself. It's real money you're giving away. Tax shelter is only those funny dollars that investors don't have to spend."

5

Kitchen Design

As you begin to design the beautiful, functional kitchen of your dreams, first concentrate all your creative energy upon the lowly electrical outlet. In addition to bringing you the power to run your machines, it is also a device necessary to the happiness and psychological well-being of your staff. Particularly the dishwasher.

Have you thought about what the dishwashing job entails? Standing under bright lights on a squishy rubber mat, the dishwasher awaits the arrival of dirty dishes from the dining room. The busboy crashes through the kitchen door, grumbling about the laziness of one waiter and demanding more clean silverware. He drops the groaning bus tray onto the stainless-steel shelf, producing a sound not unlike a pistol being discharged in a closet.

The dishwasher then goes into action. Grabbing each dirty dish, he bangs it aginst the side of the deep sink to dislodge the scraps of food, which are then washed into the roaring mouth of the garbage grinder. All dirty linen is pulled from the tray and tossed into the waiting linen bag. Dirty silverware is thrown into a pail of detergent-laced water to soak. Plates with bits of food stuck to them also must be soaked and scrubbed by hand; otherwise the dishwashing machine will merely bake the food on the plate.

A square plastic rack is set on the tray slide and the dirty dishes stacked in it. When filled, the rack is pushed into the machine, the door clanged down, and the start button jabbed. While preparing to fill the next dish rack, the operator is interrupted by the chef, who has several pans to be cleaned immediately. The pans have burned cream clinging to them like dried blood. The dishwasher turns to the deep sink. He scrubs the pans, all the while hearing behind him the feet of buspeople stacking more full bus trays on the shelf, on the floor, and on other overflowing bus trays.

At last, the dish machine finishes its cycle. The first rack is pulled from the steaming door to cool before being unloaded. The clean crockery must be carried over to the serving line, glassware put on storage shelves, and another rack quickly loaded.

Is it any wonder the electrical outlet is so important? If possible, you will want one in or adjacent to the dishwashing area, so the besieged dishwasher can listen to his radio. That's why you need to think about the outlet.

It is an interesting test of your kitchen designer or architect—and of yourself—to learn if those people understand the functions and problems of the dishwasher, as well as the jobs of the other kitchen workers. Electrical outlets for radios and for the convenience of employees using toasters, choppers, mixers, and slicers are important—not because they will make or break the kitchen, but because those small amenities make working a trifle easier.

Peter Borawsky has opened and operated several restaurants. Currently, he is a partner in a winery. Recalling his many years in the restaurant business, he says, "I've seen opinionated designers without any real knowledge of restaurant kitchens. They have no idea of what it takes to feed five hundred people."

And I have known kitchen consultants (often being paid better salaries than the people for whom they were designing work spaces) who produced designs that had no real relation to the food to be cooked and that, when scrutinized, were found to lack such essential equipment as garbage disposals.

Another test of the perceptivity and experience of your kitchen designers is to ask them where the bread will be stored. I have said before that restaurants are an accumulation of details. Obviously, stoves and walk-ins require their allotted space, but so do other seemingly small items, such as bread and condiments. Here is a sampling of items to be considered:

• Your food chopper or mixer or slicer needs not only counter space but storage space for its accessory parts. Where will they be stored when not in use? Under the grill's grease trap? Not likely.

• You will need garbage cans near the prep sink, the dish-washing area, and the cooking line. Will you design space for them, or simply place them haphazardly on the floor to encroach on aisle space and provide obstacles for people to walk around or trip over?

• Where will you store the breads, muffins, and rolls needed for sandwiches, hamburgers, etc.? Will shelves be built, or will those easily crushed foods share space with the slicer blade?

• You plan to make omelettes. Where will you put the flats of eggs, condiments, mixing bowl, and omelette pans? For that matter, where will you store your twenty-gallon stock pots, frying pans, slotted spoons, whisks, and ten-quart colander?

• You have decided that certain of your menu items, such as salads, are to be made by the food servers. Fine. Where will the salads be made—by the prep sink already overflowing with cases of meat needing to be cut, or in an alcove next to the walk-in? Where will the servers find doggie bags, extra condiments, tea bags, and salted crackers? On the shelf next to their wadded-up winter coats?

Designing a Hood

When people think of kitchens, often they imagine serried ranks of heavy-duty ranges, sizzling broilers, and fastidious, multilingual chefs turning out exquisite food. For the person who pays for the equipment, the first thing to think about is the hood. It is hard to be excited about a hood, I know. The long, galvanized or stainless-steel structure broods over the cooking line like a dormant volcano, contributing nothing to the actual food preparation and much to the cost of the kitchen.

What can the hood do for you? In addition to exhausting noxious fumes, odors, and grease-laden air, a proper hood can keep your restaurant from becoming a pile of burning embers.

Your basic hood is constructed of heavy-gauge steel and over-hangs all cooking equipment that produces smoke or vapors. It must meet stringent design and performance standards. The exhaust air must be ducted outside the building. Incorporated in the hood are grease filters, which can be removed for cleaning in dish-washing machines or deep sinks. Inside the hood and ducts is an automatic fire-control system that also has automatic shutoff valves for gas and electrical supplies. Additionally, the hood must contain approved lighting fixtures. Since air is being exhausted by the hood, make-up air must be directed back into the kitchen to compensate.

The hood must meet local fire codes, insurance codes, and the requirements of the National Fire Protection Association. As you can see, building your own hood could be very tricky. There are prefabricated models that come in various sizes. Shop around and talk to your equipment salesman. Also be sure to check the specifications on any proposals you receive. The company making the hood may not have the capability to integrate the make-up air with the remainder of the air conditioning and ventilation system. Incidentally, if the hood design for your kitchen features make-up air that will blow directly onto your just-cooked food, you should find another designer.

If the hood has no self-cleaning capability, be certain to have it thoroughly steam-cleaned at least twice a year. This is especially important in the ducts that extend to the roof. These areas are difficult to reach and are very messy. They are also the source of grease accumulation and fire. It is often preferable to hire a professional cleaning service for this job.

When designing your hood, think in terms of possible expansion. It may be worthwhile to buy a longer hood than you need now, if you believe you will be installing more equipment later.

Planning Storage Areas

All right, you're anxious to design your kitchen. But it's still not time to think about specific equipment. Let's deal first with four bare walls and a few shelves. In answer to questions about restaurant operations, an owner, an accountant, and a salesman offered their opinions about one of the greatest needs in a new restaurant:

"Even though we have a lot of unused space, we don't really have enough storage space."—Ed Moose, Washington Square Bar & Grill owner.

"The biggest mistake people make spatially is not having enough storage space. Not just for food, but for paper storage, forms, letters."—Maya Lit, restaurant accountant.

"Most people don't design in enough storage."—Ross Button, restaurant equipment salesman.

I know it is difficult to get really excited about storerooms. In fact, storerooms generally are designated after the kitchen, dining room, bar, bathrooms, employee locker room, and office have been completed. That makes a certain amount of sense, but please remember that your storage area is not merely a resting place for supplies destined for the kitchen but a depository for very expensive goods that have a direct impact on your restaurant's profits.

The receiving area is an integral part of your storage space. Although we will discuss ordering and receiving in a later chapter, I want to begin this discussion of kitchen space with the receiving area because that is the place where many restaurants get into early difficulties. People handle the new goods improperly and often fail to maintain inventory control.

The person who checks in the supplies and signs for them should not have to perform that job while making sandwiches, turning eggs, and training the new cook. Sometimes the overlap in responsibility is unavoidable. When possible, let one person concentrate on receiving and storing supplies.

The shipping invoice should be checked against the delivery and any discrepancies noted. This check should include a careful count. For items purchased by weight, such as meat, receipts should be weighed. This is not to reflect unfavorably upon the honesty of the delivery driver; mistakes can occur. The careful receiving of merchandise insures that you get what you need and that your financial statements will accurately reflect your purchases and costs.

After counting the supplies, the person responsible for them will make sure they go to a secure storage room or to refrigeration or liquor storage. In the most perfect of all worlds, only one key would exist for each of these rooms, thereby vesting absolute accountability in one person.

Ideally, the receiving area should provide space for a restaurant scale. Look into floor models that read directly and do not require beams and easily misplaced weights. Also needed is a place to store the goods temporarily while they are being checked in. The storerooms should be as close to the receiving area as practicable and as close to the kitchen as possible.

Another reason to have adequate storerooms is that you will save money on labor. It is time-consuming and frustrating to have the prep cook digging through stacks of unopened, jumbled cases looking for a single item. It takes needless time and costs money.

In this regard, there is much to recommend a walk-in refrigerator, no matter how small your kitchen. Whole cases of produce and large containers of prepped food can be refrigerated easily. A reach-in refrigerator generally demands unpacking of produce cases and careful rearrangement of stored items.

Kitchen Design Considerations

Now that you are thinking in terms of the flow of food from your suppliers' warehouses to the restaurant, we can ease into a discussion of the kitchen itself. Basically, the flow of material should be smooth and direct. Food and people will come into the kitchen from outside the restaurant and from other parts of the building.

Foods must be prepared in the kitchen. The people there must have a comfortable work area. Once ready, the food moves from kitchen to dining room. At this point, we again come back to the menu. The scope and requirements of your menu will determine, to a large extent, the kitchen design.

As much as possible, you must place related kitchen functions close together. The actions of personnel should be facilitated by design, not hampered by it; the food flowing from storeroom to dining room must go in the most direct route. Other considerations include ease of maintenance, safety, and the comfort of the work spaces.

Principal Kitchen Equipment

Since restaurant equipment can be more complicated than a child's Christmas toy, I recommend to you *Food Equipment Facts: A Handbook for the Food Service Industry*, by Carl Scriven and James

Stevens. The book is an excellent compilation of information and facts helpful in selecting kitchen equipment and in organizing a restaurant. For information, write: 9 Bilenmore Road, Troy, New York 12180.

If you have had the chance to visit an equipment supply firm, you will have some idea of the great range of playthings available to restaurateurs. With the many options, it is occasionally difficult to decide exactly how to spend your money. It is possible to buy such specialized food machines as crepe mixers, sugar-donut makers, shrimp deveiners, and automatic spaghetti cookers.

Of more practical use to a small restaurant operator is the Buffalo Chopper, a spinning-bowl machine that is like a food processor. Though it is less glamorous and less versatile than a processor, it has greater capacity and is very useful for cutting vegetables. For instance, five pounds of onions can be chopped in less than two minutes with a Buffalo Chopper. By hand, you will spend at least that much time drying your watering eyes. Food mixers or, for a small place, food processors, are equally useful. They can dice, cut, shred, and make bread crumbs.

Another functional item is a slicer. Here again, a small restaurant may not require one of the large, automatic models. A regular slicer is useful for cutting meats for sandwiches. Its ability to handle huge hunks of cheese gracefully is limited. The tube feeders for celery and mushrooms do not always produce satisfactory results.

Aside from their obvious use in making fried potatoes, fryers can speed the preparation of breakfast sausage as well as other fried foods such as breaded veal cutlets, onion rings, and seafood. Fryers are relatively expensive and not absolutely necessary to every operation. Fat is one of the most expensive components of fryer operation. Fryers are also the cause of many fires. The mechanical condition of your fryer and its thermostat should be checked often.

Grills are used for exactly what you imagine: sandwiches, steaks, eggs, pancakes, hamburgers. They come in a variety of styles for differing applications. They also have a choice of surfaces.

For many people, the image of a chef laboring over a solid black restaurant range is the essence of a restaurant. And those six-burner ranges with the large ovens are still the standard of restaurant kitchens. But the variations are endless. A typical range, three feet wide, can have six burners, or four burners and a small grill, or two burners and a hot top, or a complete hot top.

Hot tops are large metal plates similar to grill tops that fit over the burners on a range. They increase the cooking capacity of the stove by allowing more sauce pans or stock pots to be used. The chef is not restricted to using only the surface heated directly by the burner. On the other hand, hot tops cannot be used successfully for cooking individual items since there is no fine control of a separate flame.

Another cooking method you may wish to investigate is steam cookery. Steam-jacketed kettles come in many sizes. They can be used to prepare certain cuts of meat, stews, soups, and vegetables. Steam cooking generally retains most nutrients in vegetables; there also is better flavor retention than in boiling.

It is possible to plan your kitchen without including the usual restaurant range. A convection oven, steam kettle, grill, and broiler combination would be an alternative. Here again, careful study of your menu will dictate equipment.

Another possibility is a microwave oven. This device cooks very rapidly. However, some restaurant owners believe a microwave oven alters the food's texture. You should test thoroughly before installing one.

Like the steam kettle, the cheese melter has many uses. It is a distant relative of the more elaborate salamander. Conventionally, salamanders and cheese melters are used to finish food. They are used to melt cheese on sandwiches and cheeseburgers, complete

Mexican or Italian dishes, and make au gratin foods. The also can be used for seafood and broils, and can even toast bread or muffins.

Another small piece of equipment deserves mention. If you are truly intent upon making money in the food industry, forget about opening a restaurant and concentrate instead upon inventing a restaurant toaster that works consistently. Pop-ups or belts, virtually all toasters seem too fragile for heavy use. Perhaps the problem lies in the number of moving parts or the electrical components. You undoubtedly will need a toaster. Since even pop-ups are expensive, be careful in your selection.

The previous paragraphs have been intended only as an overview of principal kitchen equipment. Every item comes in a variety of sizes, capacities, and prices. It is important to assess your needs carefully, so that you buy enough cooking capacity but do not waste money on gadgets you will not use.

Leasing Equipment

Dishwashing machines are expensive. So are ice machines. Because ice machines tend to wear out faster than the accountant's depreciation schedule, and because dishwashing machines can put a big dent in your cash, check out leasing possibilities. Don't forget that both of these items require plumbing connections.

Another advantage of leasing, particularly from a company offering a service contract, is that you can be relatively certain that you will be able to keep the equipment in operation. Before you sign, try to find out what the leasing company's service representative will do when the panic phone call for assistance comes at midnight. Will he rush over to help you, or suggest that you give the machine two aspirins and call him in the morning?

Analyzing Equipment Needs

When you have a grasp of food equipment, you can begin to analyze your menu to determine what equipment you need, what you would like, and what you can afford. For example, let's say that one of your menu items is a cheeseburger. As delivered to the customer, the plate contains a five-ounce patty of hamburger, a bun, a slice of cheese, fried potatoes, a slice of dill pickle, tomato, and onion. Parsley is the garnish.

As you attempt to determine what equipment you need, follow the path of all the foods through the restaurant. The delivered meat must be weighed on a scale, then carted on a hand truck to the walk-in. Will you use a freezer to insure an ample supply for weekends and holidays? Next, the hamburger is made into patties in the kitchen and stored on trays that, in their turn, are kept where? Either in the walk-in, a reach-in, or in refrigerated drawers located under the prep table or under the grill. Finally, the meat is cooked on the grill or broiler.

While the hamburger is sizzling to a plump medium-rare, let's check on the other items that we need.

Hamburger buns are delivered almost daily, so storage requirements are not great (except those two days when you must double-order because bakers seem to believe they should have two days off each week). The bread must be close at hand, stored in drawers or air-tight containers near the food line. The buns will be warmed on the broiler or in the cheese melter prior to use.

The cheese comes to the restaurant in large blocks. After being weighed, it is taken to the walk-in. Later, it is cut into slices, wrapped, and put on trays that also are stored in the walk-in, the reach-in, or the refrigerated drawers.

Tomato, onion, and parsley arrive on the same truck in large cases. They are hand-carried to the walk-in. After cleaning, the onions are cut on the slicer, and the tomatoes are cut on a special tomato-slicing machine, which looks flimsy, costs plenty, and saves much time. The prepped vegetables are then wrapped in plastic and refrigerated.

Potatoes come in with the other vegetables but are placed in a cool storeroom. Later, they are cleaned in a potato peeler, sliced, and stored in large buckets by the cooking line. After being cooked in the fryer, they are kept warm under the chip warmer until served.

By now the hamburger is cooked. The cheese is added, and the patty is run under the cheese melter. Then all the ingredients are combined, and the plate is put on the pass shelf, ready to be delivered to the customer.

Obviously, you need not write a chapter to describe the cooking process of each food item. Simply analyze and note the equipment used in each food's preparation. Large operations may require additional analysis: Volume of sales, portion sizes, load on equipment at peak hours, and production capabilities of equipment must be figured. The small-restaurant operator will be less likely to need such a detailed study. Reference to production capabilities in catalogues will help you match equipment to your individual needs.

Designing Space

Many readers will have little difficulty with their kitchen design since they will have almost no room for equipment and no choice as to its placement. If you have a hundred square feet, your options will be pretty slim. If we assume, however, that the space does give you latitude in design, then there are a few basic ideas to keep in mind. Concentrate on the work areas. Strive for efficient, smooth traffic flow of materials and personnel.

If you have retained a kitchen consultant, be certain that the resulting drawings take advantage of the latest scientific studies concerning equipment placement, work-area dimensions, and environmental considerations. For instance, the simple selection of aisle width is a function of usage as well as the need to provide passageways. Current standards for aisle width fix 30 inches to 36 inches in operations where work is performed on one side of the aisle, and 36 inches to 42 inches when people are on both sides. If you have workers on both sides of the aisle and want to leave room for the passage of people between them, you need 42 inches to 48 inches. Measurements like these are available for virtually every aspect of kitchen design and can be useful in setting up effective working areas.

To facilitate the placement of equipment, you also should make a scale drawing of the space. Dining, storage, and cooking functions should be studied using this plan. The drawing allows you to visualize how the placement of equipment and work space will affect the whole restaurant.

Using the dimensions from catalogues or your own measurements, make templates or small-scale cutouts of the equipment. Use them in conjuction with your similarly scaled drawing of the restaurant to visualize various layouts. This step is very important since trying to locate a six-foot grill in a five-and-a-half-foot space can be quite frustrating. Play around with different configurations. Discuss the possibilities with the supplier.

Don't neglect to check your final plan against the actual space. Often, a building structural member will prevent the ideal placement of a needed piece of equipment. Be certain that what you want will fit where you want.

Stoves and broilers are heavy. Wrestling them around is tiring and expensive. While you are still measuring the space, make sure the equipment will fit through doors and halls. I have seen large reach-ins delivered at added expense by professional movers because of impossibly narrow stairwells and doorways.

You also will be thinking of equipment placement in terms of food-group preparation: meat, vegetable, bakery, salads. Of particular importance is the main cooking line, where the final product is prepared. There should be a minimum distance between the chef's working area and the pickup point for the servers. What may not be so apparent is that, although the chef is in charge in the kitchen, a certain amount of communication is desirable between food servers and cooks.

You do not want the servers wandering into the kitchen to judge the chef's techniques, but they do need a place to turn in their orders. And the chef needs a "wheel" or some clothespins and a line on which to stick the orders so he can refer to them. By having limited access to the kitchen, the servers can question the cooks about specific items, and the cooks can ask the servers to decipher their scribbled orders.

One other area requiring particular attention is that space designated as the pantry or the salad prep area or the servers' area. The name does not begin to describe all the activities relegated to this small space.

There, in an area separate from the cooking line, servers make salads. In larger operations, a prep or pantry cook may create the salads for the servers. The purpose of the area is, however, similar. A great many other tasks are centered here also. Soups are dished up, salads made, coffee and tea stored, water and ice supplies kept, bread toasted, breads and juices stored, and milk poured.

As you can see, depending upon the tasks you assign to your servers, you may need a small refrigerator, a sandwich prep station, coffee makers, dessert refrigeration, ice machines, and lots of storage. This space works best if separated from other kitchen functions. Servers can enter the kitchen, place their orders, then make salads or prepare soups out of the food workers' spaces.

While you are making drawings, do not forget to visualize vertical space. Under each grill or prep table is space for refrigerated drawers, flour bins, and small equipment. Above each table is a likely location for shelves , cheese melter, and electrical outlets. In too many kitchens, the outside top of the walk-in is used as storage, a practice not unlike sweeping dirt under the carpet.

Other Kitchen Design Concerns

In equipment catalogues, you will see pieces of small equipment from spoons to mops, from pots to pot brushes. In a small operation, many of these items may not be essential. Several can be purchased more reasonably at a local hardware store. But a couple of things bought prior to opening can save you time and energy.

One of the most important is the sturdy, manual can opener that can be attached to almost any horizontal surface. Solidly built, these openers can open virtually any can easily and quickly.

The other important item has been with us since the menu planning stages. The portion scale is indispensable for controlling menu costs and keeping portions accurate.

You also might consider rubber aprons and rubber gloves for the dishwasher. They keep the machine operator dry and also facilitate cleaning since the gloves allow dirty plates to be wiped off quickly without the need to bang fragile crockery against the sink.

Your intent in the kitchen is to build a working area that will be pleasant and comfortable despite having several pieces of equipment in full operation: stoves and grills will be very hot, exhaust-air fans rumble in their ducts, make-up air blows into the kitchen like a gale, choppers and slicers and dish-washing machines are in constant motion, pots and crockery are banged on shelves and trays, and cooks and servers loudly discuss orders, money, and baseball scores. With all that noise, it is necessary to think in terms of the best material, color, and design features to soothe the nerves of people laboring in the kitchen.

You will have a choice of wall and floor covering materials. Stainless steel or Marlite is often used on walls; quarry tile, seamless flooring, or sealed concrete are among the choices for floor construction. Compare longevity, ease of cleaning, and comfort. Also be certain your selections are approved for use by the local health department.

Your need to meet code requirements in regard to make-up air and exhaust air volumes naturally will influence the kitchen's ventilation system. Do not forget that the seasons change. You will have varying demands for providing fresh air in the summer and for avoiding drafts in the winter. You also must meet lighting code requirements. Beyond the minimum, you will find that excellent illumination pays off in increased productivity and safety.

And do not forget that after all those hours of abuse, the kitchen has to be cleaned. Personally, I favor having everything on legs. For some years, there was a school of thought favoring splash guards and skirts around the equipment. Inevitably, seams fail and cracks appear. Those small openings are fine entryways for bacteria, cockroaches, and other nonpaying guests. With the equipment on legs over a bare floor, the janitor can quickly hose down the entire area. It is also easy to see under the equipment to check on cleanliness.

Know your equipment, how it can be cleaned properly, and how often that chore is necessary. Grease traps need attention, as do toaster crumb trays, slicer components, and choppers. Learn about various cleaning methods and aids. The busier the restaurant, the more cleaning is required. The manager or chef must establish a regular, written schedule to insure that walls and ceilings, as well as equipment and floors, receive attention.

6

Construction

Dorthy Ricks owns a 675-square-foot drive-in restaurant near Kenai, Alaska. It has eight stools inside and good parking. One full-time employee prepares a menu featuring fast food for working men who have only thirty minutes for lunch. Dorthy and her husband "put it together as we had the money." It is her second restaurant: "The first place was on an experimental basis a mile down the road. The present [location] was the only place I could buy at that time, which proved to be okay. I own this land and only rented the other."

Americo's is a family-style Italian restaurant in Sacramento, California. The restaurant has a reputation for excellent homemade pasta. Partners Paul D'Allessandro and Jackson Leong built the 2,300-square-foot building by coordinating the talents of many friends and family members. They used no institutional financing. One friend drew up the plans; another helped with the electrical work. In fact, so successful was this project that the two men believe working with a large group was one of the most pleasurable aspects of the construction. They were their own contractors and only had to subcontract the plumbing. All else was accomplished through friends.

Jackie Cook has owned or operated several restaurants in California. Currently, she works during the summer as director of the Squirrel's Nest in Homewood, a resort community beside Lake Tahoe. Formerly, she and her son owned Soupçon, a very successful, though tiny, place in Sausalito, California. When Jackie talks about construction work, she talks about her son, Ford, who loves to work with his hands: "If you're in the restaurant business, it helps to have a son who can fix things."

These restaurant people constructed places without benefit of high-priced architects, kitchen consultants, or construction supervisors. On the other hand, they did not have 8,000 square feet to build, and they did have the advantage of knowing at least one person who was conversant with code requirements and building procedures.

Each restaurant and each restaurant operator have special problems. Your assessment of your strengths and needs will determine what method of design and construction is best for you. In this chapter I want to discuss certain aspects of selecting and working with architects and contractors as well as certain design determinations to be considered in planning the whole restaurant.

Choosing an Architect

Most responsible architects will tell you that the most important attribute in an architect is the ability to get along with the client. This does not mean that the architect must meekly accept all the client's ideas. But you and your architect should have a working relationship that allows for give and take. If the architect's ego and your ego are in conflict, the restaurant you are financing won't be what you want, or the difficulties of having it designed to your satisfaction will be so great that you will be fed up with it before it is built. It's no fun dreading every meeting with the person who is supposed to be helping you.

The planning stages of a new restaurant should be fun. There will be time enough for tearing out your hair when it rains the day you intend to pour concrete, or the electrician shows up three days late. But early on, you will be involved in making conceptual decisions. After considering a variety of possibilities, you can select those most appealing to you. Your creative urges, hitherto directed toward cooking and planning budgets, will now be utilized to create the design that embodies your best ideas.

To translate your thoughts into a building design requires special talent. If you possess that ability, you may not require a highly trained architect but only a draftsman to draw your basic plans. But if your talents do not include the ability to visualize a completed building, you may want a professional.

The choice is important. Spend some time talking to friends, other restaurant operators, and businesspeople. Try to locate architects who have a good reputation and who have created buildings you admire. Then go to their offices to talk and to listen. If they are interested in you as a client, they will show you photos and models of their previous work.

Perhaps you will want to know if the architect has designed other restaurants. Personally, I do not believe this is vital, especially if you have restaurant experience yourself. And if you know what you want. But if both you and the architect are rookies in the restaurant game, there certainly is a greater potential for problems.

Even if the architect has not worked on a restaurant, you can get a feel for the type of design work the firm does. Look over the company's other projects. Choose an architect whose work you like and whose personality meshes with yours.

Many architects use kitchen-design consultants, so that a lack of experience on the architect's part is balanced by the consultant's knowledge. But be careful. As we have noted before, there are a number of people in the world purporting to be kitchen experts who are not really qualified to design a sandbox.

Ned Foley owns two restaurants in California. During his years in the business, he has dealt with many equipment design firms and restaurant specialists. He warns new operators: "The people you're dealing with are out to take the money out of your pocket. They may be good guys, and they will buy your lunch, but they want to sell you stuff you often don't need." Notice that Ned is not discussing the honesty of designers and equipment salesmen, merely their need to sell you equipment. They, too, must earn a living.

George Hoover and Gary Desmond are partners in the Denver architectural firm of Hoover, Berg, Desmond. Their approach to new projects is very careful, systematic, and creative. The following paragraphs are a summary from one of their draft programs for a new restaurant.

> The purpose of this program document is to outline the needs of the project. It is crucial that planning decisions be based upon the true needs of the project. What kinds of facilities are needed? How much building will the budget buy? Conversely, what are the funds needed to meet requirements? What are the basic goals that must be met by this facility? Should the project be phased? How can new developments unknown at the time of planning be accommodated in the overall definition of the problem?
>
> The purpose of architectural programming is to ask these questions, document the answers, and thereby provide a sound basis for the effective design of the particular facility by stating the problem to be solved. This statement of the problem represents the essence and the uniqueness of the project. Furthermore, it suggests the solution to the problem by defining the main issues and giving direction to the designer.

This is the way professionals operate: define goals, discuss the possibilities in terms of function and budget, select the best design alternative, and create the best possible building. During your preliminary discussions, the architect should be offering suggestions and listening to you. It is from your dreams and the architect's creativity and practical knowledge that a synthesis is achieved.

Choosing a Contractor

A similar selection process is needed to choose a contractor. Obviously, the opinions of former customers will be very important. Like other professionals, contractors often specialize, which may be helpful to you.

Occasionally, architects will make suggestions regarding capable contractors. When Ned Foley built his first restaurant, he acted as owner-builder. The project was immense and costly. Ned says he would never do it again. In his opinion, there are too many technical details and too much that can be done improperly for the owner to be the contractor on a large restaurant.

Ned also dislikes "phasing," or "fast tracking." This is a process whereby construction is begun before all plans are completed. Sequences of construction are established and, as the plans are completed, work progresses. The method allows some shortening of construction times. For projects as complex as restaurants, it has disadvantages.

As Ned discovered, unless the plans are completely approved by designer and owner, there is a tendency to make revisions during construction. Each change is costly. Often the designer disagrees with the contractor, and the owner is caught in the middle.

I asked Les Horton for his comments concerning hiring and supervising contractors. Les has built many restaurants throughout

California and has observed much during his years as a contractor. Here are a few of his thoughts.

> The first thing your budding restaurant [owner] should be careful of is the picking of a contractor to do the work. I believe he has to be most careful of anyone he chooses, especially if he goes on a "cost plus" basis. (Contractor agrees to do all work on restaurant on the basis of cost of all labor, subcontractors, materials, etc., plus a fee or percentage.) This method is really a license to steal for an unscrupulous contractor. And the client had better be very sure of the character of the person (firm) he is dealing with. The contractor can kite invoices, submit invoices that really belong to another project, show phony time cards for labor at a higher rate than the man is entitled to and/or for more time than that man spent on the job. He can have his subcontractors submit billings for more money than his bid (remember, the subcontractor is responsible only to the general contractor, not the user) and then get a kickback from the sub and/or supplier. The biggest scam is on extras, those items of change or additions, called for by the owner because of last-minute changes in desires or needs, called for by the city because of code, and/or by the designer because of his errors or omissions. The general contractor can get almost any price he can make stand up for these items, especially if the owner is a novice in the building business.

Obviously, only a few unscrupulous contractors can blemish all contractors' reputations. Les's comments are presented to keep you alert, not paranoid. Based on his recent experience operating a construction management and consulting firm, Les has positive words about hiring a construction manager. Because many architects may not understand all code requirements, the construction manager can save the owner money by anticipating problems and by knowing how to implement architectural designs.

Les also provided advice for conducting financial arrangements with your contractor:

> In most of the Western states, the lien laws are very clear, to wit: If the owner/operator contracts for services from a general contractor to improve his property, either leased or owned, and does not pay for these services (even in cases of disputed invoices), the contractor has the right to lien the property and/or the tenant as security against payment of a debt. In other words, this law allows contractors, subcontractors, laborers, material men, or certain others who may have provided goods or services to your project, to place a lien on your business, structure, and/or fixtures that they built or improved for you, for an unpaid portion of the goods and services they furnish. For example: If you fail to pay your contractor, or if your contractor fails to pay *his* subcontractors or laborers, or neglects to make required contributions to a labor trust fund, tax agency, etc., then those people can look to your property for payment. *This applies even if you have paid your general contractor in full.*

These are the words of an experienced builder. He tells you how to protect yourself:

> The quickest and most certain method to insure that your general contractor will pay his people and that no liens will interrupt construction or opening and that the general contractor (or some other general contractor) will complete the work, is to require a performance and payment bond to cover work for which you and he are contracting. The amount of this bond can run from 1 percent of the gross contract amount to 5 percent. All is dependent on the financial security, experience, and standing of the general contractor and his relationship with the bonding company.
>
> I have heard of general contractors defaulting on jobs, allowing their subcontractors to file liens, although they al-

ready have been paid, and splitting their ill-gotten gains after the fact. Would you believe people could be so dishonest? Believe me, they can.

Designing Beyond the Kitchen

At this stage of planning, we have discussed kitchen design, storerooms, and dishwashing area. Now you need to plan your other spaces. Don't forget to use templates and scale drawings to help visualize the final restaurant. Generally, the areas remaining include:

Parking
Entrance and waiting area
Public toilets
Public telephones
Bar or lounge, if any
Dining rooms
Banquet room
Food-server areas and stations
Ice machine locations
Linen storage (clean and soiled)
Wine and liquor storage
Office
Location of safe (bar and/or office)
Employee showers, toilets, and lockers
Janitorial storage
Miscellaneous storage—additional chairs, paper goods,
    soft drinks, matches, crockery, glassware, financial
    and accounting forms, guest checks
Garbage storage and pickup areas

Government agencies naturally have something to say about your design. Previously, I suggested that you contact the city building inspector for help with code interpretation. It is useful, also, to review what the county health department might want. The following list is for "plan check," the review of restaurant plans before health department approval is given. While lengthy, the list should not necessarily be considered complete:

From Sonoma County, California, Health Department

Two sets of plans, complete floor plan
Projected maximum seating
Square footage

General Specifications:

Floor: cleanable and smooth (kitchen, storage, and restroom floors)
Walls: light-colored, smooth, cleanable (kitchen, storage rooms, and restrooms)
Ceilings: smooth, cleanable (kitchen, storage rooms, and restrooms)
Lighting: must be shown above all work areas (various minimum foot-candles of illumination)
Ventilation: hood with grease filters and fan; schedule of make-up air, hood type, duct velocity, and elevations
Water: adequate supply of hot and cold, good quality
Plumbing: schematic showing all floor drains, floor sinks, indirect sewage connections at sinks, dishwashers, food equipment, and refrigeration; grease traps outside
Refrigeration: cleanable; metal shelves, floor drain in area of walk-in box
Dishwasher: must meet National Sanitation Foundation Standard #3; floor sink
Sinks: two or three compartments, depending upon usage
Restrooms: according to occupancy; those for employees depend upon size of staff
Storerooms: cleanable; metal or wood shelves; size as a fixed percentage of kitchen area or one square foot per seat
Construction: rodent- and insect-proof
Outside refuse: suitable pickup space

Equipment: plans to show layout and identification
Cleaning equipment: a room or space outside food area for
    mops, buckets, etc.

Just as it was necessary to consider the flow of both materials
and people in the kitchen, you also have those same considerations
in the remaining spaces. Food must reach the dining room quickly
and easily; dirty dishware should have a convenient path back to
the dishwashing area. The bar and waiting areas can be adjacent to
or removed from dining rooms, depending upon your preferences
and space considerations. The important point is that the staff be
able to get to all the tables and that people waiting not be constantly
jabbed in the ribs by buspeople carrying full trays.

Necessarily, you will have to compromise. Much of your design
will be dictated by the limitations of space and the requirements of
local government. After a few weeks of operation, even the most
carefully designed restaurant spaces, such as offices, kitchens, and
lockers rooms, all begin to look alike. There are the usual bulletin
boards, empty cartons, and time cards reposing in dull metal racks.
Financial paperwork and concern for the public areas usually
consumes more hours, so that the "back of the house" accumulates
the debris of existence that is characteristic of restaurants. I'm not
saying this is a bad thing. Just be aware that your employees will
utilize these spaces in ways you never envisioned and for purposes
you hardly dreamed of.

In designing your dining room, it is obviously necessary to
review your menu to determine the type of food service. Texts on
restaurant design devote pages of information to dining room design. Also be certain to consult the local occupancy and building
and fire code for design restrictions. These can drastically affect
your design and, therefore, your estimated gross sales per seat.
Generally accepted standards fix ten to twelve square feet per

patron in banquet rooms, fourteen to sixteen square feet in dining rooms.

The selection of materials, colors, and details of design in your restaurant will be very personal. The layout of tables and servers' stations requires common sense. The idea is to create the most efficient and pleasing configuration. There must be space for the servers to move. They also should be able to see their entire section of tables from their stations. You will have to determine the number of tables and customers to be handled by each server. Although a person working near the kitchen may be able to handle one or two more tables than the server who must walk a great distance to pick up food, you cannot expect an unreasonably high number of customers to be handled effectively by one person. Eight tables of four will keep anyone busy. One more couple might bury even the best server.

In determining dining room design, it is helpful to define the duties of all employees who might be in the room. Will the host supply menus to patrons after seating them and also explain the day's special? Or will the server handle all aspects of food presentation? Will you use a cocktail server, or will all drinks and wine be brought by the food server? Where will the server go to pick up red wines, chilled wines, drinks, coffee, and condiments? Where will food orders be placed? How will the server know when an order is ready in the kitchen—via a light system like that at Dulles International, or a loud shout from the chef?

Who will be responsible for carrying food to the tables? If the busperson is going to carry salads, how can he be filling water pitchers or getting ice? After eating, will the patrons pay a cashier or the server? Will customers waiting for tables be able to glare into the dining room at people trying to enjoy a quiet after-dinner drink? Will you use bus trays to clear tables, or will you have all dirty dishes bussed on a cart? Will the cart fit between tables without imprinting a new ketchup-colored design on a leather coat thrown over the back of a chair?

As an interesting check, you might want to compare your proposed seating arrangement and number of chairs with your expected gross sales. Will your sales per person be enough to generate the gross sales you require, or do you require more seats?

It is important to have a plan for the division of labor. Just as your kitchen design was dictated, in part, by the functions of chef, prep cooks, and dishwashers, so will the placement of bar, servers' stations, tables, chairs, and cashier be related to the jobs each person must perform. Of course, you also want to provide comfort for the patron.

Your Accounting System

Let's pause a moment. You are right in the middle of worrying about all the day-to-day details of designing a new restaurant. During this time, your energy is focused upon tasks that take days or weeks to accomplish. I would like you to think for a moment in terms of years.

Since we already have determined that you are not building this place for practice, we will assume that you want to be open for a long time and that you want customers to keep coming in. You will need to account for the money. Now is the ideal time to talk with your accountant about setting up the bookkeeping system, the cash register, and cash-handling procedures.

A word of caution: Maya Lit, a restaurant accountant, remarks that, "You don't need financial statements if you're not going to look at them." Furthermore, for really small operators, there may be no need to monitor costs since the owner-chef knows where the money is being spent. "I'm an accountant, " Maya says, "but I still believe that if their [the restaurant owner's] cash is more than their bills, they're ahead."

The federal government has basic accounting requirements as, no doubt, do your state and local authorities. Ask your accountant what financial accounting is necessary. The governments want their share, so you will need sales tax amounts, income and inventory amounts, and employee payroll information. You must establish systems for keeping track of your money (and the governments' money). Find out what information you will have to record before you invest in a cash register. Then, with your accountant, analyze your intended methods of operation and the best means of monitoring those activities.

While establishing your accounting system, make a trip to a cash register dealer to see the various types of machines available. You will see the old four-button, mechanical models that require a diligent and honest operator and that sound like real cash registers, as well as the newer computer registers, which can meter drinks, figure costs, record types of sales, and emit a sound more appropriate to an auto repair shop than a restaurant.

The idea behind cash registers is not simply a totaling of gross sales but an accumulation of information that will allow you to manage your restaurant activities. A small operation probably does not require a complex system. For your information, here is a short list of some capabilities of the newer registers:

Automatic imprinting of guest checks, including taxes
Inventory control—some machines can report usage of raw
   materials as well as the number of individual menu items sold
Day-by-day reports of sales, labor costs, credit card receipts,
   etc.
Profitability of various items on the menu
Price changes made instantaneously

Many employers like the new machines because they contribute to the efficiency of the staff. Generally, there are fewer errors in calculating guest checks. There also is more efficient use of time since the machine automatically calculates what the servers once did by hand.

You should weigh the advantages of each system and consult with your accountant. Just as it makes no sense to spend money on monthly financial reports you will never utilize, it is silly to buy a complex register if you do not need its capability.

Designing All the Details

At this stage of your design, naturally you are concerned about the aesthetics of the place. We have accepted the fact that exterior design and the configuration of the public areas are matters of personal taste. Nevertheless, try to keep in mind that you want to appeal to a broad spectrum of customers. Every one is an architectural critic as well as a food critic. You must plan heating and air conditioning, lighting, floor coverings, wall and ceiling colors, height of chairs, shape of tables, textures, music and mirrors.

The impact of an expensively decorated and lavishly appointed room can be spoiled easily if your forks and knives are flimsy and improperly balanced. Will your stylish candleholders be difficult for customers to see around as they talk? You want to have mugs instead of cups and saucers, but how will you prevent the astronomical linen bills resulting from coffee stains on tablecloths? Have you actually sat in one of your dining room chairs? Is it comfortable, or does it seem a prototype for a buckboard seat?

As in all other aspects of restaurant design, the details are decisive. While you are peering at the architect's grand proposals, remember to check on the small things. Following is a partial list of items frequently overlooked by planners:

1. Public toilets should be accessible and simply designed. Check the health codes to insure compliance with requirements for the handicapped. Do not forget that you will need to keep these places spotless. Having them conveniently placed aids not only customers but busboys who must periodically check them for cleanliness during busy periods, the time when bathrooms get dirtiest and need to be tidied up.

2. Many people install their telephones near the restrooms. That is not a bad idea, but you might think twice before installing a speaker for your music system in the same area. It is not that the music makes talking on the phone difficult, but that people occasionally like to give their listeners the impression that they are hard at work. It is tough to be convincing when restaurant music is wafting through the mouthpiece.

3. Do not forget to keep a list of licenses needed before opening. Some of these permits take time to obtain, so be certain you know the deadlines.

4. If you intend to have a bar that remains open beyond midnight, or if you expect to be taking in a lot of money, you should consider a safe. It is not reassuring to make that dark walk to the night depository at 3:00 A.M. A safe—either a floor drop model behind the bar or a small office type—is convenient and relatively secure.

5. If you intend to sell cigarettes, where will they be kept? Behind the bar or in a cigarette machine? Where will the machine be placed?

6. If you are located in a region where people need coats during part of the year, have you designated a place to keep those expensive garments? Will you have a coat room, coat trees, or let the customers take care of their own garments?

7. Even though you are paying for a heating and air conditioning system that the designer claims would be more than adequate for a cruise ship, you also should consider installing air purifying machines in the bar or in rooms where people will be smoking heavily. These boxes are not all that attractive hanging from your ceiling, but they clean smoke out of the air quickly and thoroughly. In bars, where people continually smoke as they drink, the machines provide another benefit by slowing the accumulation of the brown nicotine sludge that invariably covers everything.

8. You are no doubt aware of the infinite design possibilities for your bar: simple, no-nonsense, stand-up-and-drink saloon bars appeal to most owners; others favor the round or peculiarly shaped styles that look intriguing on paper but are difficult to work. Do you have any idea what a good distance is between the back bar and the edge of the front bar? (Answer: thirty inches to thirty-six inches, if the bartenders are slim.) Will you be free-pouring, or using soda or liquor guns? Do you want a mirror behind the bar so people can check themselves, or a blank wall festooned with souvenirs from your last trip to Mexico?

We already discussed several of the difficulties associated with a liquor license. Other considerations in bar and cocktail areas include the flow of people as well as the ease of movement for cocktail servers working these areas. If you have a large bar, how will you supply it with ice, replenish beer and wine boxes on busy nights, and remove garbage?

9. Try to visualize each route your customers will take from parking to entry to table. Have you established an entryway that is comfortable and inviting? Will customers easily find the host and the waiting area? Is the waiting area pleasant, or will people feel like guests in a prison visiting room? You must create a balance here between the functional and the aesthetic, between the needs of your staff and the expectations of your customers, between the restrictions of budget and the demands of relaxing dining.

Planning the Opening

During the final phases of construction, it is time to begin preparing for the opening. There are a number of ways to announce your arrival upon the community's culinary scene. Most experienced restaurateurs advise against a grand-opening celebration, believing instead that a quiet beginning followed, if necessary, by a big event a couple of months later is preferable.

Since you are running what is essentially a manufacturing process, turning raw materials into finished products, and because the employees handling this complex job are subject to human frailties, it is a good idea to keep your first days low-key. This gives everyone, including you, a chance to learn the best working methods.

Peter Borawsky constructed a restaurant in a small Oregon coastal town. He budgeted almost $10,000 for pre-opening publicity. His reasons make sense in the context of a new operator entering an unknown market. He invited virtually every important individual in the town, as well as club members and civic organization workers, to open-bar, buffet dinners. In a town of less than 10,000 people, it was a good move, for it gave the cooks a chance to prepare all the menu items and provided valuable publicity.

Earlier in his restaurant career, Peter had helped to open another place in Palo Alto, California. The community there is much larger and more diverse than in the Oregon town. To invite all the prominent people would have required the Stanford University stadium, which is nearby. Instead, Peter contacted a civic organization noted for its charitable work at Stanford's hospital and held an open house at the restaurant for members of the organization and their spouses. He provided an open bar and buffet for twenty-five dollars per couple and sent every dime of money to the charity. It was an opportunity to familiarize the clientele he sought with his operation and to garner free publicity.

There are less elegant ways to conduct pre-opening dinners. A few years ago, I was invited to an opening dinner where guests were encouraged to make comments concerning the food. It became very evident to all but the most obtuse that the owners did not really want to hear anything negative. The cliché, "It was good," brought smiles to their faces. The word "but" sent them scurrying to another table.

The place lasted for a while and was taken over by new operators, who sought to take advantage of the pasta craze. They invited 250 of what charitably could be called their closest friends, then added 250 more guests. They had to stagger the feeding. The pasta approximated the macaroni and cheese I ate as an undiscriminating child, and the drinks came in plastic cups. Silliest of all, in their attempts to invite almost everyone who could have been anyone, the new owners forgot a whole group of the town's "old money," thereby triply defeating themselves through sloppy thinking, improper planning, and mediocre execution.

By the time you are ready for the pre-opening dinner, the staff should be trained in the fundamentals. The first night should not be a "right stuff" test wherein you attempt to push the limits of the staff or the guests. You want to polish techniques, smooth the rough edges, and discover those small details in preparation and service that need attention.

If you must be masochistic and ask questions of your guests, ask specific questions. Was the wine properly presented? Was the meat correctly cooked? Why did they think the Baked Alaska was actually Cherries Jubilee?

Remember, too, that your guests will have preconceptions and may not understand what you are trying to do. That is not necessarily their fault. If the patrons do not share your goals, do not assume they are dolts. Maybe you are not communicating very well.

In a small town not far from San Francisco, a six-month-old restaurant was visited by the owner of another establishment in the same town. One of the entrees evidently was marred by an improperly prepared sauce. When this possibility was suggested to the chef, he responded that, alas, one of the difficulties he was having in the town was educating people's palates!

Plan the pre-opening dinners carefully. Most of your friends undoubtedly will be excited about your new project, so avail yourself of their enthusiasm. Let them eat free and pay for the meal with intelligent criticism.

7

Hiring and Supervision

Most restaurants have a personnel office the size of a file drawer. Musty as an old spy's office, the drawer might contain a few ancient employment application forms, dated notices from government agencies regarding employment procedures, and a few scraps of blank paper. Because the restaurant owner is interested in food, customers, and decor but not in employees and their problems, the drawer usually remains closed, and the restaurateur continues to ignore the needs of the workers.

Yet supervising employees and handling the paperwork associated with personnel duties often require many hours each day. The work demands your best efforts. I consider the staff of a restaurant as vital to its success as the food. They are definitely as important as the owner.

Evaluating Your Own Skills

Before you begin to evaluate others, it might be a good idea to take a look at yourself. I have no doubt that you may be one of the most charming, intelligent, and ambitious individuals in your community. But can you cook? Or run the dishwashing machine? Or pour a good drink? Do you understand the proper and most effective methods for cleaning lettuce? For doing setup work in the dining room? For cleaning broken glass from an ice bin?

Before supervising, you have to understand what you are responsible for. As I have mentioned before, operating a restaurant requires many talents. If your operation is small and you have some restaurant experience, you should be able to devise systems for cooking, serving, and cleaning that will suit your place. Lacking experience, you should seek help from those who have the knowledge, hire someone who has done it before, or be very good at thinking through every step of any procedure.

You will be hiring people to perform all manner of jobs in your restaurant. Unlike a General Motors assembly line, in a restaurant it is possible to learn, if not master, the basics of every position. You will be a better employer and a more astute personnel supervisor if you know the work requirements for each job.

You also will be better able to evaluate job applicants' strengths and more effectively fit the good people into your operation. Your restaurant will have many details needing attention, and being able to recognize, hire, and retain good people will ease your worries about many aspects of the operation. You then can concentrate on facets of the business that are not going so well.

Since we are discussing your qualifications, not those of your employees, we should start by analyzing supervisory functions. I always have believed that a good supervisor can lessen much of the grief associated with the restaurant business. The manager or owner who anticipates problems, who works with an intelligent plan and with thought, will not avoid difficulties but certainly will have fewer surprises than the crisis manager, the person who waits for a problem to arise before acting.

This concept is particularly true in regard to personnel. As the owner, you are going to expend a great deal of money and energy to hire the best people. After they are trained, you would like them to stick around. And you would like to have them working to help the place, not just because the money happens to be good or because it is a place where a clever thief can advance in his chosen profession.

The way you treat your staff will be reflected in their attitude, in your employee turnover rate, and ultimately in the number and type of customers sitting in the dining room. Because the subject of personnel management is as complex and potentially costly as the space program, I would like to talk about it in relation to specific problems. This certainly will not be an exhaustive discussion. Its purpose is to get you thinking about the impact of your personality and habits upon your restaurant's staff.

Supervising Employees

Much of supervision is common sense. In fact, successful restaurateurs often use that term to describe the manner in which they manage. But dealing with people is tricky. One person's definition of common sense is frequently another's idea of lunacy.

As we have determined already, restaurant owners are real go-getters—self-starters who are assertive and aggressive. This means they have to be especially careful in their handling of employees. The same characteristics that make a good entrepreneur are not necessarily good in a personnel manager.

All of us have encountered the hard-as-nails type who runs his operation by fear: "If they don't like it, they can take a hike." It's an interesting concept, perhaps suitable for military boot camps, but only those employees with large debts and families are likely to work for long under those conditions.

Do you enjoy being bullied? If so, I doubt you will find anything to agree with in these pages. If you have children at home, you may be trying to teach them to use the words "please" and "thank you." Use these words in your restaurant. Tough talk and sarcasm are not the way to go.

Remember, too, that your employees depend upon you for their jobs. Much as they might like you and enjoy the work, most of all, they need the job. Consequently, they are watching you, testing your mood, alert to the slightest variation in your disposition. If you think I'm kidding, try to remember back to a time when you had a job you needed. Did you perform it any differently and did you feel differently when the boss was around?

As supervisor, you expect your floor people to leave their personal problems at home, so that the customers sense only sweetness and light radiating throughout the dining room. If the staff must not be moody or sullen or irritable, why should you have those rights? Look at it from an economic view. If you upset the staff, your customers will sense the tension. If the mood is happy, your customers will be happy and will want to return.

But lest you fear that I've gotten softheaded, let me balance the card by saying that my management philosophy is based upon a couple of four-letter words: "Firm but fair." After all, even if you have to be in a good mood, you still have to make intelligent decisions.

The corollary to my management principle goes like this: "Every employee, regardless of position, believes himself to be the hardest worker in the organization." Your job as owner-supervisor is twofold: Even if you believe the corollary applies to yourself—that you are indeed the hardest worker—don't tell anyone; and treat your staff fairly, so no one has reason to complain or to believe you do not appreciate their work.

Let's look at the chicken and egg question. You built the place, so the staff would not have jobs without you. Without them, what would you have? Remember the ego! Those people who receive, cook, serve, bus, and clean are people who deserve to be treated fairly as individuals. Once again, think of the economics. If employees produce more by being treated better, then business logic would seem to indicate the appropriate policy.

Before your first employee begins work, think about what supervisory techniques you will use. If you are a small operator, your place will be evolving all the time, and you will have a chance to get to know your staff. A larger restaurant requires a more methodical approach. What are you going to do if many of your workers are high school students who all want time off to go to the senior prom? What will be the standards for determining who gets which shifts? What will you do about a waiter beloved by the customers—and by you for his conscientious approach to the job—who antagonizes his fellow workers and causes your chef to reach for a cleaver each time the prima donna enters the kitchen? How will you go about proving that an employee you once trusted is stealing from you?

You won't believe the infinite variations on a theme that can be worked by restaurant employees. They do not fit molds. People who work in restaurants are notoriously strange. Accept it and work with it. Don't try to change it. Only a maniac—or someone who liked the work—would spend eight hours a day in a hot kitchen or behind a busy bar. It would drive anyone to drink, and has.

The floor personnel and bartenders might be a little whacky and might talk too much. So what? Your customers don't want an undertaker waiting on them, and you don't want your business to resemble a funeral parlor.

I cannot emphasize too strongly my belief that next to food, the staff is the most important part of a successful restaurant. There are as many varieties of restaurant workers as customers. It is the owner's job to hire the best—no easy task when you consider the working conditions and hours.

I have worked up a list of subjects that often require attention and can be a continuing source of vexation for supervisors:

1. Before you open, call or write the local, state, and federal government offices in charge of labor laws. They will not help you run your business any better, but they can advise you about your rights and obligations as well as the rights of your employees. There are laws regulating virtually every aspect of work. If you are using union workers, you will have another set of regulations to think about.

2. You want to be in charge, right? Can you empty the grease trap? Start the fryer? Find the bar? Some time before or shortly after you open, you must learn how your place operates. Mind you, I don't advocate that you become the resident expert at all these jobs, but I do suggest that you, or your manager, know what each job entails. Once you have done the work, you will not be so panic-stricken when somebody quits or when you have to fire someone.

3. That waiter who has been pocketing tips, the cook who refuses to do the prep work correctly, or the host who cannot treat customers decently is hurting you financially. You must rid yourself of the non-producers—for your sake and for the good of the productive employees.

You say you have never fired anyone before? It's easy if you are callow and vindictive, in which case you will be doing the employee a favor anyway. But if you are at all aware of the vagaries of the human condition, then often there will be doubt and always there will be an awareness that in most instances the employee is not so much a felon as simply a personality who does not fit into your operation or mesh with the other personalities on the staff.

I am an advocate of intensive training to integrate new people into your place. Effective training can eliminate many potential problems. The probationary period, when new workers are still learning their jobs, is the time to determine their suitability. It is disheartening to have devoted many hours to developing a good employee only to discover that it is not working.

Correcting faults requires patience. If you have spent time trying to correct a worker's weak points, and the job still is not performed well, don't lose your temper and carry on in front of other employees. In fact, if the worker is big and strong, you shouldn't lose your temper at all. Furthermore, there really is no excuse for a supervisor to flare into anger. You may well dance around the edges of anger now and then, but really big explosions are not effective unless they are for an extremely good cause.

Occasionally, it is difficult to juggle the schedule after you have fired someone. Still, it is better to have other people work more shifts than to delay the action. I also believe it is counterproductive to fire at the end of a shift. If you have made up your mind, call the employee in or meet him at the front door when he arrives for work. Then go to the office. Review the history of problems (which you have written down and will keep as a record), have the final paycheck made out, and do it. There is no way you won't feel bad. But later, when your entire operation is running more smoothly, you will be happier.

Of course, with any luck, you may run into an employee such as the one Jerry Mulrooney, head waiter at a San Francisco restaurant, found: "The guy had only been working a few days, but he just wasn't making it; so I took him aside and give him the news. It didn't even phase him. He said, 'The reason you're firing me is that I'm young, good-looking, dynamic, and aggressive. And the other employees are jealous of me.'" There is no comeback for that one.

4. Employee meetings give no one joy. In a business of details, such as a restaurant operation, it is essential that everyone be kept informed of policy changes, new menu items, and problems or jobs well done. Most meetings are a waste of time, however. Employers call them at their convenience, not necessarily when the staff has something to say.

In a small place, there is no need for meetings; the give and take of daily operations will reveal problems and solutions. But larger restaurants with big staffs usually require meetings.

Do not expect the staff to love this kind of meeting. For some, it will fall on a day off; for others who are working before or after the meeting, it will merely mean a longer shift. But the time together can be productive if the employees feel free to express their views. Listen carefully at meetings and be flexible. You may have an employee droning on interminably about some pet project. Even if the general idea is unworkable, listen. Maybe buried in that long monologue is an idea you can use. At least the orator has been thinking about your operation. If nothing else, it indicates a healthy interest in the place.

By the way, employees are generally entitled to minimum wage for attending meetings.

5. Don't forget details in the restaurant. Every single item, from the tops of salt shakers to the grill on a compressor motor, requires attention periodically. And like people, the tiny details will respond admirably to kind attentions.

A restaurant owner who can carry on a conversation in the dining room or kitchen and look the listener in the eye for more than five seconds is not watching details. You need eyes quicker than an infantry scout's, and your awareness of your environment should be just as acute. Burned-out lights, dirt on ledges and baseboards and table bases, a broken latch, overcooked meat, wilted lettuce, dirty pour spouts, or smudged mirrors all detract from your place. Think of any part of your restaurant, and you will be thinking of something that should be looked at regularly if not daily, then weekly or monthly.

Don't sit in the same place each time you eat. Move around. See what the customers see. A shelf that looks clean while you view it from a standing position may have crud adhering to its bottom, which is visible only from the level of a seated customer.

The attention to detail will pay off. Not only will your place be cleaner and better maintained, but if your staff knows you care about the details of their work, your food and drink will be more carefully made and served.

6. Consistency of preparation and service are a function of management supervision and attention to detail. Your customers are not coming to your place because they want to be surprised. Sure, new food items are wonderful, but the old standbys have to be made the same way all the time. Hence the need for detailed recipe cards and a quick supervisor's eye.

The customer is paying in anticipation of eating a certain style of food. Customers return because they liked the food last time. Give it to them the same way this year.

7. Let's imagine that you are out sailing on your new yacht. Naturally, this dreadnought is named after the successful restaurant that has financed it. A couple of lines are frayed, and the mast is slightly bent. How well can this boat be sailed? Well enough to stay afloat, no doubt, but not the way it was intended.

How, then, can you expect your cook—who is back in the bowels of your kitchen—to perform perfectly when the thermostat on the stove is erratic or he is short of stock pots? The dishwashing machine needs a pre-rinse unit. Did you go to the plumber yourself, buy the unit, and bring it back to put into operation, or did you merely call in an order on your way to the yacht basin?

Your staff needs the proper tools to do their jobs well. They take it personally if you know about a problem and do not take care of it. And they should be offended—it means you don't care.

8. The government will mandate many of the rules for the welfare and payment of your staff during working hours. But you will set the vacation policy. Make it easy for people to get a rest; they will come back much refreshed and much happier. Even owners need time away. Ed Moose of the Washington Square Bar & Grill maintains that for him the worst part of the restaurant business is not the long hours but the struggle to stay fresh. He tries constantly not to let the stream of customers become a burden or a source of irritation.

Owners use various methods to structure time off. Some favor a maximum of four shifts per employee per week. Others do not limit the number of shifts worked but require that everyone take a week off every two months.

If the money is good in your restaurant, you will find that most employees want to keep working until they begin to look like death march survivors. Beware fatigue. The constant pressure of working with the public adds immeasurably to the tension of restaurant work and can lead to early burn out.

9. Remember people's birthdays.

10. As you no doubt understand, your employees are not working for you out of love. They need the money. Despite what you may consider lavish wages, the majority of their income will come from tips. You can handle the disposition of tips any way you want. Be sure to check with the state and federal governments and your accountant about laws regarding tip credit on salaries, tip reporting for tax purposes, and the handling of employee tips.

The whole subject of tips should, if possible, be decided before you open. Many places allow each server to keep the tips they earn. In others, all the servers pool their tips and divide them equally. Generally, the buspeople receive a cut also—from 10 percent to 15 percent. In other places, servers share tips with hosts, bartenders, and kitchen staff.

I happen to be a great believer in pooling tips. It prevents isolationism. People are encouraged to help each other on the floor because everyone benefits. There also is less fighting for position when it is time to assign stations.

Incidentally, the federal government does not approve of tip pooling except among servers, buspeople, and dishwashers. If you are concerned about the legality of your tip system, check with the local Department of Labor office.

How to handle tips is not an easy problem to resolve, but once your policy is set, changing it will cause more emotional upheaval than the Civil War. Think it through, talk it over with everyone, and be careful.

11. It is not true that the customer is always right. In fact, if a complaint is delivered with arrogance and hostility, the customer is definitely out of line. If the same problem is discussed politely and dispassionately, then there is cause for recognition of the customer's point of view.

I would be the last person to say that restaurants do not make mistakes. However, the handling of complaints, if done properly, actually can increase your business rather than injure it.

Be sure the staff understands your policy for handling complaints. In many cases, the customer and server cannot agree because the root of the problem is in their antagonistic stances. Probably the safest method is to call the manager or owner immediately. If the complaint involves food and has even a hint of validity, swallow the old pride and buy the meal for the person. A former restaurant owner, Van Bagley, believes that one unsatisfactory ten-dollar meal actually can cost a hundred dollars in losses, since the disgruntled customer will tell everyone he knows about how lousy your food is.

To handle complaints intelligently, you must know your product. Know how the food should taste and look; know what wines taste like. If a customer refuses a bottle of wine you know is fine, ask what the customer wanted. Then offer an alternative to the refused bottle. I have seen customers reject three bottles of the same wine because they did not know what they were looking for in a wine.

It is also essential that the staff know you will back them up when things get sticky. No worker should have to take abuse. The man who says to the bartender, "Serve and be servile," should be at home, not in public—and definitely not in your restaurant.

The employees should know that as long as they are doing their jobs well and within your guidelines, they will be supported. A big spender has no more excuse than an obnoxious drunk to take advantage of employees. I have known customers who had a problem with an employee and cited, in defense of their actions, the amount of money they thought they spent every month in the restaurant. Uusally, their imagined expenditures could have supported us for a year, not a month.

As you begin to collect larger numbers of regular customers, you also will begin cooking items you did not know were on the menu. That is because some people have genuine dietetic needs that should, to the extent possible, be catered to and others have psychological needs for recognition that you also must acknowledge.

Of course, this can lead to the "Me too" ordering syndrome. One guy gets a special order, and someone at the next table wants it too. You have seen the same interaction among children. Your job as owner is to handle the special orders with tact and intelligence.

12. In a business characterized by rapid employee turnover, it is to your benefit to retain good people as long as possible. You are not running a restaurant training school. The idea is to hire and keep the best. If you are looking for longevity in the business and not merely for the fast buck, it may be worthwhile considering regular raises, profit sharing, and fringes such as health insurance for the staff.

It won't take much to make your place different. In return for a little extra care of the staff, they will take care of you. They will be an extension of you. Theirs will be another set of eyes looking for problems, not trying to ignore them.

The customers will be happy too. Restaurant patrons are conservative. The dining room or bar is an extension of their living room. They enjoy seeing the same faces and the same good food; it enhances their sense of well-being. In short, by working for retention of staff, you are making your job easier and your restaurant better.

Hiring Staff

Staffing your restaurant prior to opening may present problems. You must have your job descriptions established. That may be difficult if you have never waited on tables, cooked, or even worked in a restaurant.

Where are these people to be found? If you know someone you trust who has restaurant experience, you will be wise to ask their advice. But remember that what works for one person may not work for you, so stay flexible. Also be sure to institute good security for food, money, and other valuables. You don't want your new employees surprising you with their nimble fingers.

Employment agencies are a decent source of help. They often charge the employer a fee and do not always vouch for the quality of their applicants. Newspaper ads work, but you may be deluged with people you cannot or will not use.

Local vocational schools or cooking schools are a source of help also. However, if your operation demands a certain level of maturity and experience, you may have difficulty finding qualified students.

You can find simple job application forms at your local stationery store. Or make your own. You do not need a lot of detail. You will want the usual name, rank, and serial number, plus an address and phone number—restaurant employees need a phone; often there are shifts that need to be covered on short notice. A complex application cannot tell you anything that you can't better determine in an interview.

The exception is, of course, employment history. And a listing of former supervisors. If you can contact a previous employer, you will have a good source of information. But please remember that restaurant employees do not fit into easy categories. They may not make good middle-level managers in a utility company nor necessarily be able to sit through three years of law school, but that does not mean they will not be good food workers. In fact, they may have an advantage.

Van Bagley required applicants to write their reasons for applying at Van's restaurant. That might appear to be an exercise in which a good fiction writer would excel, but Van also asked the same question in the interviews. He was able to compare the answers and provide a way to get the applicants talking.

How much previous experience is necessary? There is no answer. Early in the operation of your place, someone who has learned a great deal from another restaurant can be an asset. Later, when you know more, that same person might have habits learned elsewhere that do not fit into your method of operating.

Naturally, little of the above applies to kitchen personnel. Unless you have the leisure or the small size that permits you to train people in handling knives, slicing mushrooms, boning chicken, and all the thousands of other skills cooks must have, you may be very inclined to value previous experience.

Before scheduling an interview, call previous employers and references. Find out the nature of the business, the duties of the applicant, and if the applicant would be rehired. Even if the answer to the last question is no, do not necessarily write the person off. Inevitably, there are two sides to these stories. If you are still interested, it may be worthwhile to follow through with the interview to hear the applicant's version of events.

On the other hand, simply because a former employer would rehire doesn't indicate a desirable employee. How do you know the first employer is competent? Maybe after you hang up, he'll call his attorney to declare bankruptcy.

After you have studied the applications, you are ready to interview. If you are hiring for a night operation, it might be worthwhile to conduct the interviews at night. The interview starts when the applicant appears at the door. Use all your senses and try to detect the true character of the applicant. Since you will be talking to people who may be trying to outguess you, ask technical questions: What were your duties at your previous jobs? How did you perform *x* or *y*? Cooks particularly need to be quizzed about methods and skills.

As you gain experience and become more adept at interviewing, you will devise the kinds of questions you feel are most useful. Since many of the applicants I interviewed were likely to be involved in theatre or writing, I usually asked them to talk about that aspect of their lives. It gave me a good idea of how serious they might be about working in the restaurant. Other possible questions might be: What previous jobs did you enjoy and why? What do you dislike doing? What do you do in your spare time?

Dan Mulrooney is a waiter in a busy San Francisco restaurant. He has trained untold numbers of new people and developed definite ideas about what to look for in an applicant: "You're looking for honesty and hunger. That means somebody who's enthusiastic and willing to learn. There's nothing more irritating during training than having a guy tell you he has a better way to do something."

Dan also asks applicants about their plans for the next year. By the time you calculate your time and costs, your training program takes a good hunk of change. Having a new employee complete the entire training period and then quit because his parents want him to run the family pool hall can cause you unnecessary grief.

Hunger, the desire for work, can be discerned. It is seen in the person who is willing to take any position to start if there appears to be a fair chance of advancement. It is evident in questions about what the job involves, not how good the money is. And it is apparent in the applicant willing to return for a second interview and not in the boy who wants to be sure he can have enough time off to see his girlfriend.

After a time, it will become easier to spot the real workers. But hiring will always be an art that no amount of testing and no computer can ever make easier.

Training New Employees

Training begins with the interview. During that first meeting, the broad policies and philosophy of the restaurant should be outlined, pay scales discussed, and training schedules explained. Every employee should be hired with the understanding that for a given period of days or weeks a probationary routine is mandatory. That time allows you to watch the employee's development, and it allows the new person to learn more about you and your restaurant.

Many establishments put trainees on special pay. For instance, a flat "casual labor" wage for the first shift worked, then 10 percent of tips collected while training (one to two weeks), then 15 percent during the final stages of probation (perhaps another three to four weeks, with a review session by supervisors before going on full tip cut).

Not only is there financial incentive in this type of program, but this method also reminds the "recruits" that they don't yet know it all. For the inexperienced, a good month on the floor is often necessary for real proficiency. In the kitchen, a graduated pay scale can accomplish the same goals. After a probationary period, all employees should be technically equal and therefore entitled to full pay.

There are many approaches to orienting new employees. Try to remember that they are not like a broiler to be plugged in and fired up. A personal introduction to other staff by the supervisor and a brief orientation period by that same person will help immensely. A most important aspect of orientation is an explanation of policy. It is maddening for both the employer and the new employee to have the employee learn piecemeal about various policies that long-time workers take for granted.

Steamer Gold Landing restaurant has a checklist of items that the manager discusses with each new employee. The list does not cover every possible question, but it is more effective than relying upon the manager's memory for all details:

History of restaurant	Employee meals and prices
Names of owners and managers	Two-week notice and rehire
Walk-through of restaurant	Employee attitudes
Restaurant philosophy	Uniforms and grooming
Hours of operation	Rest breaks
Entertainment	Punctuality
Full menu description	Smoking on shift
Customer relations	Eating, portions
Customer complaints	Telephones
Reservation policy	Restaurant property
Credit cards	Parking
Check-cashing policy	Work schedules
Identification procedure	Schedule changes
Third-party liability	Employee illness
Time clock and pay	Underage employees
Tips and tip pooling	Employee charges
Tip declaration	Deliveries
Vacation pay	Paychecks
Group health insurance	Employee meetings
On-the-job injuries	Errors
Training manual	Two-week training schedule

After orientation, many restaurants issue new workers a training manual the size of a city phone book. I doubt many are read cover to cover. Before the first session, the new employee might be given a sheet with a description of menu items to learn and a price list to memorize. It is helpful to list for them the items, such as pen and wine opener, that they should bring to work. Actual techniques for serving, running credit cards, handling tips, and writing tickets are easier to learn by doing than reading.

Jerry Mulrooney and his brother Dan work in the same restaurant. Jerry, too, has trained many new employees. His goal is to make them technically proficient. His method: He has the new person follow him through the first couple of hours on a shift; then he turns the station over to the trainee.

Jerry says that the most important and often most difficult idea to learn is to "finish off a table." That means every task which can be finished at one table is to be completed before moving to the next table. Like the football player who begins to run downfield before he is sure he has the ball, a waiter who is working on one table but already worrying about the guy across the room is certain to foul up both tables. Finish one off, then move on.

As owner, you will establish your own systems for taking orders, writing abbreviations on food tickets, serving cocktails, and bussing. There are no set methods for achieving these goals. You must learn to adopt the most efficient system for your individual place.

After each training session, the trainee needs a review and a summation. Jerry writes out his comments to be certain they are remembered. One of the most elusive skills to be acquired is a relaxed manner. A food server who is natural and at ease will readily adapt to the different personalities at each table. The nervous or rushed server never will be able to create a comfortable, relaxed dining atmosphere.

Jerry seldom phrases his criticism of technique in humanitarian terms. He refuses to say that it is necessary to perform a certain task because it will help another employee or make the customers happier. He talks instead about self-interest. To do a job in a specific manner may save time, that is the important point. In a busy restaurant, it is not charity but the instinct for self-preservation that keeps employees above water.

In addition to helping new workers become technically proficient, you must instill in them an understanding of their place in the overall operation of the restaurant. Try to insure that everyone appreciates the problems associated with other jobs.

Some people will be hired who quickly demonstrate a total incapacity for restaurant work. The place in which Jerry works is extremely busy. He recalls one trainee: "He'd just taken over the section from me. I looked around and couldn't see him. I went to the kitchen, but he wasn't there. The guy had disappeared. I went back to the station. Naturally, it was a shambles, so I put on my apron and started trying to catch up. I happened to look down the bar, and there he was, having a beer. I went down to ask him what happened, and he said, 'Are you kidding me? It's way too busy. I could never handle it.' He finished his beer and left!"

Until you are operating your own dining room, you will have trouble visualizing the dynamics of a room full of hungry customers. One thing you and your staff must be aware of is the customers. That seems to be another of those obvious statements. What I mean is that the assumption should be made initially that the customer is decent and understanding until proven otherwise. Yet many restaurants become very enamored with their own success, or very complacent. It often seems they would be happier if the customer would simply mail in the money and not bother showing up for the meal.

You must instill a continual awareness of the customer. If a party arrives at the door and the host is not there at the moment, someone else should have the initiative to fill in until the host returns. You have gone to a lot of trouble to get the people in the front door; it is no time to be coy.

Nothing sets people on edge like being ignored in situations where they wish to be acknowledged. Simply telling customers that they will be attended to momentarily can defuse more nervous energy than a Valium. The same is true after they have been seated. If the server is busy, a quick acknowledgment of the customers' presence will help ease their wait and make them much easier to deal with.

And how about a simple "goodbye" when diners leave? The suave host, the proficient waiter, the glib wine steward can all be forgotten if, after the patron pays his bill, they treat him as though he were a convicted child molester. Let the customer know you know he is on his way out the door. Tell him thanks for the business. He may be back.

8

Daily Operations

After all the difficulties associated with opening your restaurant, you may be excused for wondering what could possibly be more trying than those early days. You have spent long hours planning and thinking about design and equipment. You have haggled with contractors, worried until each phase of the project was completed. You have done the best job possible in staffing your restaurant with personable, intelligent people, and you have given them good equipment with which to work. Your books are virginally clean, awaiting the first totaling of sales, which will be needed immediately to keep the banker, the baker, the government, the landlord, and the suppliers off your back.

At last, after long months of work, you have begun to serve food. Suddenly, you are faced with a whole new set of responsibilities. You must order, store, and prepare food every day; supervise your staff; maintain cordial relations with customers; clean and repair your equipment; keep the restaurant in top condition; and, after a long day standing over a hot stove or a cold host's station, you must work on the books, making up bank deposits and insuring that there is enough for the government and everyone else.

No doubt you have heard endless stories about the high mortality rate of restaurants and the chances for your financial demise. Restaurants fail for precisely the same reasons other businesses fail. There are many possibilities, including too little start-up capital, inexperience, and lack of familiarity with the product. Restaurants undoubtedly are more prone to an early demise simply because they are, by their very nature, extremely complex, requiring a wide variety of skills and knowledge.

Jackie Cook is an experienced chef who believes there is at least one other reason for restaurateurs' troubles: "I don't think people are willing to work around the clock anymore." She may be forgiven for a slight exaggeration, but she does make an excellent point. If you go into business for yourself, you cannot expect to work a straight forty-hour week with time off for good behavior. This is particularly true of restaurants, with their longer operating hours and their demands for behind-the-scenes work. You are going into business for and with yourself. You will have long hours. The assumption is that you will be working at something you enjoy, surrounded by people you like.

In Logan, Utah, Guy Cardon runs the Bluebird restaurant, an establishment founded in 1914. When Guy's father and a partner, M. N. Neiberger, began the Bluebird, they cooked a portion of each day's food in their homes. They did not recognize a distinction between the workplace and the home. They struggled through the Depression with help from friends and neighbors. Today, the Bluebird seats four hundred customers and employs sixty people.

The restaurant business does appear difficult. You must control a product that spoils easily; the inventory turns rapidly (up to fifty times per year for some items); and you deal with the public, whose tastes and desires never can be predicted. Your job is to attract and please those people, feed them well, and keep yourself solvent. It is a complicated but by no means impossible task.

"I don't think the restaurant business is as tough as people make it out to be," says Peter Borawski. "Look, once you've got the customer in the door, he's yours. It's your job to sell him! You've got him there; all you have to do is show him how good you are."

Peter's thoughts are echoed by Sam Jarvis, owner of the Metro Bar and Cafe in Portsmouth, New Hampshire. Like the Bluebird in Utah, his cafe has been in operation almost seventy years, having been founded by his father in 1913. Sam emphasizes the need for flexibility and for an awareness of the surrounding community's desires. To broaden the Metro's appeal, he recently remodeled and even redesigned his logo. The change has been well received by his customers. In conversation, Sam exhibits a concern for the patron, a realization that, "If they have given us the consideration of coming to the restaurant, we have to be ready to go. We have to entertain these people. We are hosts and must satisfy them."

The purpose of this chapter is to discuss the daily operation of a restaurant. Obviously, every detail of the job will not be illustrated. I do hope to touch upon many subjects that will require almost daily attention from you.

Although many of you will have a liquor license, I have reserved discussion of bar operations for the next chapter. Even though most aspects of liquor operations are similar to other restaurant procedures, the handling of liquor and liquor-consuming patrons is sufficiently peculiar to warrant a separate discussion.

Ordering Supplies

We already have mentioned that aspect of food that makes those boxes in your storerooms different from the items on the shelves of your local shoe store. Food spoils. As a consequence, you will be ordering supplies several times each week and must constantly plan ahead to avoid overbuying or being caught short. And while you need not be overly concerned about temperatures in the dry storerooms, you must watch the walk-ins carefully. A broken freezer condenser or an improperly adjusted thermostat can quickly destroy hundreds of dollars in inventory. Since you are dealing with a perishable product and since you cannot expect to store large quantities of any items, you can easily understand why it is essential to have professional, reliable suppliers and why you must learn to order well.

I assume that sometime during the building of your place, you made contact with food-service suppliers. You may have used them to help with the purchase of an opening inventory, so you already should have a good indication of their capabilities. Naturally, large houses such as S. E. Rykoff offer advantages in shopping since much of what you need will be on one order form. But as in other aspects of business, largeness and supposed efficiency may not be solely important, especially to you, the owner of a small restaurant. Freshness of goods, frequency and time of delivery, or even the personalities of a supplier's employees may favor the smaller supply firm.

In your search for suppliers, do not neglect specialty products. Many small places handle unusual items that may be ideal for your menu. Particularly in rural areas, you can find people willing to provide products from the back of their trucks or from small farms. I am not suggesting that you devote all your time to looking for the best tomato grower in nine counties. The large firms may well have tomatoes when your small operator is sold out. But if you can find authentically fresh chicken, or a few pounds of locally raised lamb, or fresh blueberries, perhaps you can fit those into your menu.

It is vital to you that the supplier's representative be competent. The rep must understand your operation, keep you apprised of any price changes, and offer you specials while they are still special. Being a salesperson, the company representative undoubtedly will be affable enough. But does the rep know what is going on in the food business? If a freeze has damaged Florida's citrus crop, will the rep warn you and suggest alternative sources, or look dumbfounded when your next order comes back from the warehouse marked "out of stock"? Does the delivery driver make an effort to arrive at the hours you request, or do you find the truck doubleparked in front of the restaurant at noon? Since not all restaurateurs are perfect, will the sales rep personally deliver on Friday afternoon the essentials you forgot to order, or will your phone call be answered by a machine telling you that the rep is unavailable until Monday because it is, after all, almost the weekend?

When you visit the supplier's place of business, you will notice that the firm has warehouses. You probably do not. Let this fact suggest to you the desirability of having the supplier do the warehousing of goods. Do not tie up your money in inventory. You will want adequate, not excessive, storage. There is an opinion popular among restaurateurs who have small storerooms. They believe it is actually beneficial to be short of room since the buyer is less tempted to purchase too much or to make special buys on foods that are not needed.

Be careful of those "good deals." To be certain that a quantity discount will benefit you, it is necessary to analyze prices, usage, and storage availability. If you will save money by purchasing a large amount of olive oil but lose money because the storerooms are so small that the oil has to be moved constantly from corner to corner, then you will be wasting the money you saved on oil by paying for the sweat of the workers who must lug the cases back and forth.

Maggie Carlson owns a small, franchise restaurant in Northern California. Having little practical experience when she bought the place, she depended upon the previous owners and her suppliers to help with the ordering—not the best policy. It took Maggie almost a year to learn the intricacies of accurate, timely buying. Now she is comfortable with the task, but she did not enjoy the education.

With luck, you will not require that much time. But remember that food purchases directly affect your food costs and hence your profits. It is to your benefit to learn all you can about buying.

We have come many pages from our early discussion of menu planning. Once again you will readily understand that your menu determines how, when, and what you must order. If you have prepared a menu consistent with your best ideas, the chef's cooking abilities, and the availability of food supplies, then you should have no problems. If, however, you intend to serve boar meat or other exotica and the only source of supply is a company located miles away, across the Mason-Dixon line, then you may have difficulties.

In planning the menu, you developed specifications for each product. Now you have placed your orders based upon those specific requirements. When the food arrives, will you know what is in the cases? Have you been supplied with the proper items and been properly charged? Produce often comes by the case, or by the number of individual items (the count) per case. Fish is sold by weight or by count. Cans and containers vary in size. In ordering, you must know and specify what you want.

To facilitate ordering, you need to plan ahead, which means looking behind. Keep a record of past sales, the weather, holidays, and any unusual events. By predicting what your sales might be, you can order more effectively.

Another aspect of intelligent buying is accurate record keeping. Most operators make lists of items by category, such as dry goods, meats, fish, dairy products, and produce. The individual items within each category are listed alphabetically, and each is identified as to size and packing specifications. As orders are placed, they are recorded on those lists.

After a few months of operation, you will know what quantity of each product is best to maintain. That number is the "par number" and represents your best estimate as to how much of the item you need consistent with usage and storage. On your order form, you will have a place for the date and columns for each item, listing the par level (also called "build to"), on-hand amounts, and amount ordered.

Once you have placed and recorded the order, do not throw the order sheet away. You will use it to check against the invoice when the delivery arrives. The price, quantity, and quality of your groceries should correspond exactly with what you requested. The decision as to how thoroughly each delivery should be checked is yours. Some restaurateurs prefer complete counts. Others simply spot-check. You are trying to insure that you get what you want and are paying for.

Many owners even add all the prices on the invoices before signing for receipt. If you find discrepancies, you should have a good system for insuring credit. That might be a simple memo to the company asking for credit, along with copy on the invoice. The important point is that any item shorted or spoiled or missing, but charged on the invoice, must be accounted for.

Storage and Inventory Control

The most effective means of insuring inventory control is to give only one person a key to the storerooms. A receiving clerk responsible for storing and issuing all food is your best method of security. If you want no control, have a set of keys that floats from person to person, or simply leave the storerooms unlocked.

Accountability is vital to inventory control; yet many places are too small to have the luxury of a single clerk. Here again, as is so often the case in discussing restaurants, it is the owner who must decide upon security and accountability as they affect efficiency and quality. Remember, the ideal is total security and total control. But don't forget that the real purpose of your operation is to get food to the customers.

To prevent abuse of your good nature and your expensive goods by little rodents, air and water contaminants, or improper temperatures, you must keep the storerooms in good condition. This is not so hard if, as in the kitchen, you follow a clean-as-you-work rule. If you prefer to let dirt and empty boxes accumulate for a couple of weeks before cleaning, you may find yourself playing host to all manner of insects and pests. Peculiar storeroom odors floating through the dining room are likely to unsettle customers.

Do not try to save on electrical bills in storerooms by using twenty-watt bulbs and issuing miner's headlamps to workers. Good lighting helps, as does prompt and accurate marking of all containers. Each restaurant will devise a system for its own storage spaces. Marking and labeling the products and noting the date received will speed the search for specific items.

After all goods have been checked in at the receiving platform, they should be promptly moved to storage. This is particularly important when partial, or "broken," cases arrive. Anyone strolling by the case can casually palm a loose, pocket-sized product.

In the storerooms you need a system that enables you to keep track of what you have. A sheet similar to the order form, itemizing inventory by category, is useful. Another method is to utilize individual inventory cards for each item. No matter which system you use, you will want to have a record of each product, the purchase date, and the number received. A notation for withdrawals is essential also. By recording the amount on hand at inventory time and accounting for all receipts and issues, you can make easy spot checks.

Also, don't forget to train your staff in the principles of stock rotation. The rotating of stock requires constant supervision. It can be a laborious process, especially in confined areas with heavy cases. With each delivery, the older goods must be shifted to the front of the storage shelves and the newer items stored behind them to insure that the older products are used first. Having adequate storerooms that are larger than foxholes eases the burden of moving, stacking, and restacking goods.

Once again, let me urge you not to forget the local health department. Undoubtedly this agency will have regulations controlling the storage as well as the cooking of food. At the outset, try to establish good relations with health officials. Even though you have a highly developed and carefully cultivated pride in your restaurant, you should leave that pride on the coat rack when the health inspector arrives for the monthly visit. The inspector can easily close you down for violations or make your life miserable by forcing absolute compliance with every rule. On the other hand, these officials are a fine source of information and help, so it is to your benefit to deal with them positively.

Once you have managed to haul all your goods into the storeroom and to bar the door, the cases and bottles and boxes are pretty safe, if you have good key control. But having your supplies locked away does not help your kitchen do its cooking. You also must devise a careful means of issuing from the storerooms to the various departments requiring stock. Larger operations try to have one issue per day, calculated upon projected sales and past volume. The chef fills out an order form, with a copy for the kitchen and one each for the storeroom and the office.

The goods then are taken to the work centers in the kitchen, where supervisors or the chef assumes responsibility. Since you know what has been issued and can calculate from guest checks what has been sold, you will have some control over the food used in the kitchen.

Additionally, many restaurant owners take daily closing inventories of major items, such as meat. As part of the closing routine, the manager is responsible for a nightly count of expensive items. This involves another piece of paper, but if you are worried about control, it may be worth the effort. This nightly inventory should list all goods to be counted, the amount brought forward from the previous day, the amount prepped that day, a par count, a closing count, and the number sold that day as determined by a guest-check count. In this way, you will have an instant comparison of items on hand, sales, needs for the following day, and any missing items.

From time to time you will have to open your storerooms to issue food which inadvertently was not ordered by the kitchen staff because of oversights or requisitioning errors. The occurrence of these "forced issues" can be reduced by having a chef's closet that is handy to the kitchen and that is stocked with commonly used foods.

Your control of stock and of food freshness also will be enhanced if you do not become unduly distressed when a menu item is not available ("86'ed," in the jargon). Better to run short occasionally than always be overstocked with foods that spoil or that must be reused in specials of dubious originality.

You have to count all your stock at least once each year to keep Uncle Sam from getting after you. Most operators take a physical count at least once a month; many prefer weekly or daily counts in certain departments. Inventories are vital determinants of food costs. They are seldom entirely accurate. Depending upon annual sales, discrepancies in inventory amounts of a few hundred dollars can move the food-cost percentage up or down a percentage point.

Use two people to count—one for the manual work of pointing

and adding, the other for the clerical job of recording the numbers on the inventory sheet. Although your inventory sheet may be arranged alphabetically, it is better to take the actual physical count according to the order in which things are stored in the room.

These elaborate accounting and security procedures are necessary because food and liquor stocks have an unfortunate tendency to disappear when people are around them. This seems particularly true in establishments with a large staff. You can't check on everyone's morals, so try to reduce the temptations.

Many restaurateurs periodically change the locks in sensitive areas. Keep locked those doors that are supposed to be locked. Check the back door and garbage areas of your restaurant. Innocent-looking discarded boxes may contain many dollars worth of transportable and delicious steaks. Insist that boxes be broken up. Many employers peer into employees' satchels and packages. However, before you begin playing at being a customs agent sniffing for contraband, check with your local authorities to see who can do what to whom. Keep an eye on air-conditioning ducts; they provide snug hiding places.

Fundamentally, I believe that if you treat your staff honestly, they will respond in kind. Unfortunately, not everyone is susceptible to kindness, so it is up to you to lessen their chances of going south with your property.

Supervising the Kitchen

Once the food has reached the kitchen, the responsibility for its preparation, security, and cooking is the chef's. Here, proper training and good supervision can pay dividends to the owner. To control costs and provide customers with the best possible meals, it is essential that the food be expertly and expeditiously handled. In the kitchen, the basis for this handling is the standard recipe card or a bound recipe notebook with plastic-coated pages. On the cards are listed all the ingredients, amounts, and preparation procedures for each menu item. These cards should be complete, handy, and up-to-date, so there is never any excuse for improper cooking.

Each worker in the kitchen must be well supervised to insure that proper trimming, weighing, and preparation methods are utilized. During the actual cooking process, more supervision is necessary to see that correct temperatures and cooking times are employed. The safe use of equipment must be insured. It only takes a few words to list these requirements, but the jobs themselves and the attendant supervisory responsibilities are constant, ongoing tasks.

Do not assume anything. Every time you go into the kitchen, sample something different. Talk to the staff to determine if they understand what they are doing and where their jobs fit into the food-prep sequence.

In most smaller restaurants, the chef is also an owner, so the final cooking and arrangement of food on the plate is handled by someone with a vested interest in the restaurant's success. Still, the kitchen offers innumerable opportunities for error. A cold supervisor's eye is needed.

Frequently, cooks will exhibit a tendency to think for themselves. This isn't bad if they run their thoughts past you for approval. It can have disastrous results if their thinking is counter to yours or if they believe their approach to food presentation is preferable to yours. Encourage thought but also demand communication. If someone has an idea, it should be discussed with a supervisor, not unilaterally implemented.

Of course, your job as kitchen supervisor does not end when the plate leaves the kitchen. You must watch over waste also. Vegetable tops and cuttings can be used in soups or as garnish. Meat bones can go into soups or stocks. Meat trimmings can be used in stews or casseroles. Creative use of leftovers and end products can reduce your food costs while contributing to an innovative menu.

And don't forget to provide detailed, written instructions for cleaning and closing after the shift. It is the supervisor's job to insure proper cleaning of the kitchen, intelligent utilization of work time, and control of break and rest periods.

Daily cleanup in the kitchen begins with the staff cleaning as they work. Spills and stains should be wiped up immediately and floors swept periodically, not only to keep the kitchen cleaner but to prevent the crud from being tracked throughout the restaurant. It is also good P.R. to have a clean kitchen even during mealtimes. Delivery drivers, sales reps, repair people, and visitors see your kitchen. It is good for you if they can tell their friends that the place is clean, not that it regularly looks as though your sewer line had backed up.

Unless your menu is confined to frozen meats cooked in a microwave, you will find grease and scum building on walls, ceilings, and shelves faster than interest charges on your bank loan. Behind the toaster lurk forgotten pieces of bread that may require a crowbar to dislodge. Scraps of meat, left for a couple of days in an improperly cleaned slicer, will remind you of their presence with a pungent aroma not unlike that of the grease trap you have forgotten to clean.

Following is a suggested cleaning checklist. The frequency is really a function of your volume, tolerance for dirt, local health-department regulations, and your staff. Personally, I prefer clean kitchens. A well-maintained kitchen is like a fine piece of equipment—purposeful, functional, and a pleasure to use. A dirty kitchen primarily reflects the failure of the supervisors.

Daily
    All cooking equipment
    All food-prep areas
    Coffee machine

Dishwashing machine and area
Floor and floor mats
Hood grease filters
Food-receiving area
Reach-in
(Naturally, all public areas are cleaned daily.)

Weekly (one, two, or three times each week)
Walk-in
Grease trap
Shelves
Outside of hood
(Windows and mirrors in public spaces)

Monthly (more often if necessary)
Walls and ceiling
Inside of hood
Storerooms
Steam exhaust ducts (every six months or as needed)

An added advantage of a clean restaurant is that it inhibits the spread of insects and rodents. Cockroaches will arrive, freight paid, in cardboard boxes and other conveyances. Mice prefer the subway route through holes in foundations or through open doors. Flies are often so numerous they seem to travel by jumbo jet.

All these visitors are controllable. All may require the attention of a professional exterminator. People who tolerate an occasional fly or spider at home get incredibly incensed to see the insects' cousins dining at a restaurant. The more you learn about these pests, particularly cockroaches and rodents, the better you will be at refusing to let them board with you.

While you are concentrating upon food and staff supervision, do not neglect the equipment. Even in a small operation, there should be a file folder kept on each major piece of equipment. Warranties, service records, repair calls, and costs should be recorded. In many towns, it is possible to contract for monthly servicing of appliances, refrigeration equipment, and heating and ventilation machinery.

To cook well, it is necessary to have well-maintained equipment. The thermostats of ovens, ranges, and broilers are subjected to punishing use. They must be calibrated at least monthly. To maintain proper temperatures, the coils of refrigeration condensers must be clean. The upkeep of older equipment is a constant challenge. Proper training and regular preventive maintenance schedules can eliminate many problems.

Energy conservation is an integral part of equipment usage and maintenance. Every restaurant operator should strive to use energy-effective procedures and to buy equipment which minimizes energy use. The subject of energy conservation is complex but vital to the profitability of your place. Your local utility company can evaluate your energy usage and suggest means of reducing costs. Your library will have several books on the subject.

Heating, cooking, and ventilation use most food service energy. In the old days, every piece of equipment was started early in the morning and continued to operate throughout the day. Now, start-up times are staggered, the equipment is turned off during slack periods, and cooks strive to cook with maximum efficiency.

Many companies manufacture intriguing devices to help you conserve energy. Walk-ins have plastic strips called energy screens over the door to retain their temperature even when the door is open. In-line water filters reduce electrical usage by making equipment more efficient, and special heat recovery units utilize the heat generated by ice machines when making ice.

Being conscious of your energy usage and striving to conserve will benefit you financially. You would be wise to learn about this constantly changing aspect of restaurant operations.

Even though we have followed the progress of the food from receiving point to the cooking line and are about to transfer responsibility to the servers, one more aspect of kitchen control must be mentioned. When pricing the menu, you determined portion sizes for everything that is served. To control food costs and restaurant profitability, these portion sizes must be followed. Cooks and servers must have properly sized ladles and accurate portion scales. They must be trained and supervised in portion control.

Just one or two excess ounces of soup served over a week's time can add significantly to the cost of doing business. It is the owner's responsibility to be certain that proper serving techniques are utilized to control costs and waste.

The control of food requires that all food leaving the kitchen be accounted for. Usually this is accomplished with a two-part guest check. After the server takes a customer's order, a carbon or soft copy of the guest check is given to the chef to initiate the cooking process. The cooks use the soft copy for reference while cooking, then place that copy with the completed order. Before the food is carried from the kitchen, the server checks it against the soft copy, then returns that copy to the chef.

Ordinarily, the guest check has space for the server's initials, the date, the table number, and the number of customers. All this information should be filled in, as it is important for cost control and menu analysis.

While we are still talking about food as a physical substance to be intelligently handled in the kitchen, do not forget the proper storage of dressings, breads, lettuce, and other items that may remain unused overnight. Plastic wrap and care in cleaning the pantry can save money. All employees must know their responsibilities. The old line, "It's not my job," can result in waste at the end of the day. Similarly, carelessness and delay in serving the food are costly. You need an expeditious means of notifying servers when food is ready to be served. And servers must be taught to get the food quickly to tables. Correct ordering procedures, efficient work areas, and good work habits will reduce errors and losses.

Supervising Dining-Room Employees

Just as the physical appearance of food is altered by its passage through the kitchen, the essential nature of the product is again altered in passing from kitchen to dining room. Our concern for food as a physical entity changes, for now we are asked to oversee its proper presentation in a comfortable atmosphere.

In addition to caring for the physical inventory, we must manipulate mood and setting. The food is transformed from a strictly physical substance, which requires weighing, cutting, and cooking, to an aesthetic creation providing not simply sustenance but sensual pleasure and emotional contentment.

The supervision of dining room employees naturally emphasizes their physical duties. Nevertheless, their activities are judged not solely by the quality of the food and service, but also by the mood that they create and foster. When asked about his reasons for continuing to work at San Francisco's Blue Boar restaurant, Georg Isaak emphasizes his regard for his fellow workers: "Going to work every night is like going to a party with fine people. It's fun." This is true of many restaurant workers who enjoy their fellow employees as well as the customers.

Relating to Your Staff

For employers, there is another side to personnel. Sandy Saxten, co-owner of Kimo's in Lahaina, Hawaii, and Jake's at Lake Tahoe, California, believes that the worst part of owning a restaurant is personnel problems. Similarly, Ray Martin of Las Cruces, New Mexico, regards "food and labor control—getting people to care" as his major concern.

The restaurant is your dream, and you have the most incentive to work at it. You may be unreasonable to demand that the employees participate to the same degree in that dream or work for love. The supervisor should explain the goal, outline the means of attaining it, and insure that employees follow that plan.

If your staff did everything exactly as required, you would not be needed. Try to remember that people work for more than simply money. Sure, they work with you because they need to eat, but they also are interested in more subtle objectives and in satisfactions that may have nothing to do with their income. People work for recognition, responsibility, challenge, and growth.

By its very nature, a restaurant cannot always cater to those desires. That is the reason many restaurant workers lead other lives as artists, real estate agents, or musicians. They like the financial opportunities offered in food service but draw their identities from other activities.

Still, the owner's attitude and sensitivity toward the staff is important. Unfair or unintelligent supervision, really poor pay, unhealthy or unpleasant working conditions, or lack of job security can sour anyone and destroy any concern for the place or the job. Providing each employee with personal satisfaction is absolutely necessary.

Effective supervision requires effective planning. You must be able to define the job and then train employees to handle it. You must establish guidelines, policies, and procedures, then implement those practices. In a small restaurant, your staff naturally will be closely involved with the operation; you will turn to them for advice. Employee involvement is no less important in a larger establishment. Participation is more difficult, however, since large places usually are more rigidly structured.

You must be concerned about the working conditions of your staff. Pay attention when the prep cook tells you that the garbage grinder sounds as though it has swallowed a brick. Take an interest in the staff's mental health also. If a normally enthusiastic worker seems listless or depressed, you might nose around to discover if personal problems are the cause.

Talk to each employee. Let your staff know you are available for consultation or just conversation. That brief chat in the morning gives them a sense of your presence and you a chance to check on both their attitude and their appearance. Taking the restaurant's pulse pays off in increased employee participation.

Preparing To Open

So, let's say you are at work, ready to supervise. The question is, what do you watch for? Work in the kitchen is quite straightforward. The cooks' job is to prep and prepare food, clean as much as possible while they work, and perform general cleanup after the shift. Naturally, your menu will dictate the sequences, methods, and timing. The menu has influenced kitchen design, cleaning, and operations. Your handling of food, its storage, issuing, and preparation, is circumscribed by the health department and your own rules.

As we also have noted, once the food leaves the kitchen, it becomes more than a mere physical product. To enhance the healthful, visceral characteristics of food, your dining room must be clean and your staff well trained.

Before each shift, while the cooks are preparing for the next meal, your servers must complete various preparatory tasks necessary for the efficient, orderly presentation of food. They might arrive for work an hour or more before you open to the public. Their setups might include stocking the pantry with lettuce, dressings, salad condiments, grated cheese, lemons, coffee, tea, and crackers. Cleaning the pantry and servers' stations also is required. Following is a list of typical setup responsibilities:

For each server station:
    Clean station surface
    Clean coffee warmer
    Refill ketchups and mustards; wipe down outside, lip, and
        cap of each container
    Stock bottled sauces (e.g., Tabasco and Worcestershire)
    Stock water glasses, coffee cups, and saucers
    Stock wine lists, menus, artificial sweeteners, sugar
        packets, matches, toothpicks, ashtrays, and straws
    Fill salt and pepper shakers
    Stock tip trays
    Fill stapler
    Change date on credit card imprinter

In each section:
    Wipe down chair seats
    Set up tables with tablecloth, napkins, silverware,
        flowers, salt and pepper shakers, ashtray, and matches

Additional side work:
    Wipe down all ledges (Monday and Thursday)
    Clean all photos and wall decor (Tuesday)
    Wipe down all table bases (Wednesday)
    Empty, wash, and refill salt and pepper shakers (Friday)

It is a good idea to require that everyone be prepared to open five minutes before the actual opening time. This provides a little buffer for the usual forgotten tasks. It also gives the staff time for a couple of deep breaths before the customers arrive.

Overseeing the Floor

Once the first people walk in the door, you no longer can worry about the light that is burned out, the crumbs scattered on the chairs, or the dirty tablecloths piled in a corner. The servers must now begin to work to the standards established and maintained by the owner. The task of waiting on tables can be as straightforward and casual as dining at home or as complex and stylized as a ballet. The manner in which customers are served and the surroundings in which they are seated are an important influence upon people's choice of restaurants.

In large cities, where lunches and dinners are taken in restaurants three, four, or more times per week by some people, informal service with excellent food might suffice on all but special occasions. In smaller, suburban towns, where dinner out is often an event to mark special circumstances, there may be a need for more formal presentation. Of course, the city dweller may require the same sense of formality when celebrating an anniversary or birthday, while the citizen of a small town may take lunch in a sandwich shop five days a week.

You must control all aspects of your food service. Are the servers efficient, making every trip to table, station, and kitchen useful, or do they stroll languidly about the dining room, their hands empty as their heads? Do they finish each table before moving to the next, or do they jump from task to task and table to table? Can they open wine bottles and still carry on a conversation with the customer, or does the cork await removal until the punch line is delivered?

It is not just the efficiency of servers that must be monitored. All aspects of the job should be scrutinized. Are the servers concerned with the cleanliness of their stations? Crumbs on a chair, food particles clinging to a fork, or a wrinkled napkin thrown casually on the table can upset a patron's enjoyment of an otherwise decent meal.

Have you trained the servers to present the wine and food exactly as you wish? Do they follow your instructions? Innovation among servers on the floor can be just as destructive to your ideals as that among cooks.

Food service is composed of a hundred tiny moves. The restaurateur must select those that best reflect his vision. Have you thought through the way in which food will arrive at the table? Carried by each server? In a serving cart? By conveyor? By helicopter? Do you want a rigid sequence followed when serving tables (e.g., babies first, then juveniles, then women and men)?

How well do your servers monitor the progress at each table? Are coffee and water containers kept filled? Is the guest check presented in a timely manner, or does the server wait until the people are hungry again before going back to the table? Is it easy for customers to pay the check? I personally prefer to be informed by the server or by a notation on the guest check where I am to pay. I dislike wandering around unfamiliar restaurants looking for a nonexistent cashier.

Relaxation on the floor is vital. If, after several weeks, a server is still nervous in his work, you should consider finding a different position for him. Nervousness in a food server is about as welcome as a social disease—and almost as communicable. Customers want to relax. If the server cannot relax, no one in the room will be at ease. Up to a point, relaxation can be learned. Beyond certain limits, the perpetually nervous should be considered for work not involving restaurant customers.

Many operators devise elaborate manuals for food servers. Obviously, a chain of restaurants needs to have virtually everything codified to maintain its image. Small operations may get by with one or two typed pages of procedures.

It is important to have all necessary information written down and available for reference. That way servers can check on the number of mustards for each station, the size of highball glasses, and the correct setup routines. But only proper training by another individual can make a good server. Like skiing, food service is an activity that can be minutely described in a book, but beyond the fundamentals it needs to be practiced.

While we are discussing serving techniques and the servers' manual, note that there is a school of thought that prescribes much of the conversation between patrons and servers. Personally, I do not enjoy this rigid approach to serving. But it is your restaurant, and the choice is yours. However, there are two phrases that I think are worth utilizing. The first is employed at the end of a meal, when it is time to pay the check. To avoid confusion, anger, or embarrassment, I believe the server, when picking up the money or credit card, should repeat the amount of the bill and the amount of money being offered—for example, "Six dollars out of twenty dollars." In this way, both server and customer tacitly acknowledge that a certain amount of money or a credit card is changing hands and that something may be expected in return.

Secondly, I believe that when orders are turned in to the kitchen, they should be accompanied by "Order, please," not the abrupt, "Order."

Beyond these basics and within the bounds of propriety, I think servers should be allowed to exhibit their own personalities. You will find that many customers do not want to have any conversation with servers but want merely to be fed. Others will ask for life stories or anecdotes. If you trust your employees to determine the appropriate behavior, I believe you will have a more comfortable place.

As supervisor, you also must watch the performance of buspeople, hosts, cocktail servers, and door people. You must be sure that they follow the procedures you have established and trained them in. Does the hostess smile at new customers, or greet them like a traffic cop? Can the host look at a face and remember it, or does he need a mug shot of each customer? While waiting for a pot of coffee to brew, is the busboy using his time to get ice for the bar or to talk football with the dishwasher? When you go to a waiter's station, are you greeted by the anxious faces and waving arms of people needing everything from drinks to the check? Is the busgirl still relatively clean after a full shift, or could she be mistaken for a walking bus tray?

There also are responsibilities the servers should not be expected to bear. Among these are the approval of personal checks and house charges, the determination of promotional sales, and the verification of mistakes in drink or food. In your own operation, you may discover other functions that, for reasons of financial control, you prefer to have you or a manager approve. Complaints of any sort should be handled by the supervisor.

To maintain control of food costs, the first step is guest-check control. The books of checks should be locked away and a record kept of the numbers issued to each server. Errors involving guest checks, such as walkouts or food items improperly ordered, should be verified by the supervisor.

Guest-check sales representatives usually can tailor the numbering system to your needs. Servers must turn in or account for all guest checks issued to them. The used checks should be compared with the carbon copies that have gone to the kitchen. You want to be certain that the food that left the kitchen was paid for and that the restaurant, not the server, received the money.

There are several methods for controlling the issuance of guest checks. Some restaurants give their servers an entire carton of checks, making them responsible for that batch. Others issue only a few books of fifty guest checks each. Every server must account for checks not used or not turned in.

Cash register companies often can supply you with a convenient form for recording the checks issued. Some restaurants run a felt-tip pen diagonally down the side of each book of guest checks before issuing it. When the checks come back, placed in numerical order by the server, a quick glance to the side of the stack indicates a missing number.

Restaurants also supply their servers with a daily envelope for recording all transactions. A sample form might look like this:

Daily Sales Summary Sheet

Name _____   Day_____   Date_____

    Guest check numbers issued   #_____ to #_____

    Guest checks returned   #_____

    Guest checks transferred

       to (server's name)   #_____ to #_____

Sales (information from guest checks)

Dining room food sold $_____

Dining room liquor sold $_____

Dining room wine sold $_____

   Subtotal $_____

   Sales tax added $_____

Tabs from bar $_____

                 *Total sales $_____

Receipts

Food house charges $_____

Liquor house charges $_____

Food mistakes $_____

Customer charges and tip $_____

Promotion $_____

   Total charges $_____

   Credit cards (including tip) $_____

   Cash collected $_____

                 *Total receipts $_____

*Starred totals should agree

There are innumerable variations of this form. The important point is to account for all tabs, sales, and receipts. In consultation with your accountant, design the server checkout envelope for your requirements. And don't forget to devise a system for handling the money after you close. Some people make up a deposit for the bank night depository; others have a safe in the restaurant. Strive for a daily deposit in your bank.

While the servers are closing out at the end of the shift, you might stroll around the now-empty restaurant to see how well they have performed the closing duties. Are there clear guidelines for the care of leftovers from the pantry and servers' stations? Who insures that coffee warmers are off, lights off, creamers returned to the reach-in, and bus trays emptied? Who makes the final check before the kitchen crew is dismissed? Who checks the locks on storerooms, walk-ins, and office? Who handles the servers' envelopes? Who locks the front door?

Overseeing Labor and Food Costs

During the time that you observe and supervise the staff in your restaurant, you also are directly overseeing your labor costs. For many people, the phrase "overseeing labor costs" conjures images of dour little efficiency experts scurrying around the place with charts and stopwatches, timing to a hundredth of a second each person's movements. That is not what I mean.

You should be aware that the cost of labor is very high. In recent years, labor, as a percentage of the cost of doing business, has increased rapidly. That is not simply because wages have risen, but because of all the other costs associated with payrolls. When we talk about labor costs, we include not only wages but many items that are associated with, though not themselves, labor costs. For instance, we must count vacation and holiday pay, meals, Social

Security payments, workers' compensation insurance, health and pension plans, and bonuses. As you can see, the cost of serving a single salad is much more than the labor of cutting the lettuce. Although you may not expect to own a multi-unit chain with a cast of thousands, you should be prepared to analyze your labor and scheduling systems to utilize the staff most efficiently and economically.

Traditionally, many types of workers in the food industry receive federal and state minimum wage. The assumption is that their tips will provide the difference between a living wage and starvation. In some states, a tip credit may be applied against the minimum wage. There are specific guidelines that your state labor department and the federal Department of Labor can explain to you. Be careful to comply with these standards, as failure to do so can cause you untold agony should a disgruntled employee file a grievance against the restaurant.

Labor costs are directly related to hiring, training, and supervising. If you do not select the best people for the job and then train them thoroughly, you already have lost the labor cost battle. No matter how good your supervision, it cannot compensate for mediocre talent. The normally high turnover rate of restaurant employees naturally increases labor costs because of the continual expenditures to recruit and to train.

You must strive to develop good work habits. Most employees will not come to you as perfect workers. With effort, you can make intelligent employees better contributors to your restaurant.

Knowing the job and knowing how to schedule effectively also saves money. Effective scheduling involves an awareness of the restaurant as a dynamic organization having busy and slow periods, daily and hourly variations. A record of past sales can aid in scheduling.

Of course, most restaurants have an absolute minimum number of employees. No amount of juggling can reduce that number.

The employees needed for more than the minimum tasks are subject to scheduling manipulation. Be particularly careful of overtime dollars. They can quickly ruin a budget. Also be certain to evaluate your hours of operation. It is entirely possible that you are not adequately setting your opening and closing times to coincide with the rhythms of your community.

While we are discussing labor costs, it is worthwhile to devote a few words to the subject of financial analysis and control of your restaurant. Labor costs and food costs—those are the major variables that must be watched. Your accountant and a couple of the books listed in the appendix can help you better understand your financial statements. I believe your accountant will provide the most help. Remember, the control of costs is vital. You will become more familiar with the variables each day you are open.

If you recall the discussions on menu pricing, I mentioned that several pricing methods were available to restaurateurs. I also suggested that after you had been open for a short period of time, you would have more data for controlling costs. The information you extract from the financial statements—actual cost percentages changes in sales volume, rate of growth—will be dated. It may be several days from the time the data is collected until it is processed.

Hence, the need to use simple, day-to-day checks to monitor costs. You will want to know which items are selling best, what contributions each makes to your profit, and what a change in the sales mix can do to profits.

One important management tool is the sales count—the total of each menu item sold during a particular period. This number can be obtained from the guest checks. A tiring process, it nevertheless does give a good basis for appreciating which menu items are providing revenue and which are not, for knowing which foods are popular and which could better be tossed out with the dishwater.

It is possible to make your daily count sheet quite detailed by grouping together those foods that have similar food-cost percentages so that you will have a better indication of how your costs are altered by differing sales mixes. A change in the mix can have a decided impact upon your food-cost percentages. Also remember that after the sales figures are obtained from the guest checks, those numbers can be compared to the daily kitchen inventory sheets for major food items, thereby providing a crosscheck of inventory counts.

Another figure to compute is the average customer guest-check amount. This is simply the average amount of money each customer spends in your restaurant. It is a useful number for analyzing and pricing menu items. Again, in consultation with your accountant, you can learn to understand your financial statements and, in conjunction with other information derived from your daily operations, to utilize those records in controlling costs and planning future operations.

Insurance

As you look through your list of costs, one that is subject to much control and a source of much irritation is insurance. You have invested a lot of money in your restaurant, so it makes sense to protect that investment. Although you can buy insurance to protect you against almost anything, as a restaurant owner, you are interested in certain specific categories.

You certainly will want liability coverage, protection against lawsuits claiming damages or injury because of normal operation; probably workers' compensation, depending upon your state's labor laws; and comprehensive coverage against losses by fire or other disasters that damage the building or its contents. Other types of insurance include business interruption, flood, plate glass, life, automobile, sprinkler leakage, and a health plan for employees.

You definitely will want liquor liability coverage, which protects you against claims for damage caused by drunks or minors who, after drinking in your place, go into the world and run over people or into property.

Theft

There is another type of loss that can ruin your plans, deprive you of sleep, and take all the fun out of owning your own place. Pilferage, stealing, theft: words describing the act of taking what belongs to others. Remember, pilferage costs you money.

We already have discussed ways to provide security for your purchases. The use of order sheets, inventory cards, break sheets, daily spot checks, and daily sales summaries certainly will lower the chances of food walking out the back door.

A positive means of reducing the incentive for theft is to establish fair employee prices for meals and drinks. Most restaurants provide one meal per shift for their workers. The staff may order off the menu, or the chef might prepare a daily special. If the workers are allowed to order from the menu, usually they are given a meal allotment: For instance, they might be permitted to order anything on the menu without charge, up to a price of five dollars. If they decide on more expensive items, they pay the difference between the higher price and their maximum allotment plus sales tax on that difference. Employee meals also are used for wage and tax purposes; consult with your accountant on this subject.

By offering employees drink prices that are adequate to meet your costs, yet are below retail prices, you are providing them with an immediate, tangible benefit above their basic wage. Unless the staff is composed of alcoholics, you will not lose much profit with this system. You will gain much good will from your employees, who understand your operating costs and appreciate your efforts to give them a break on liquor.

Security in the front of the restaurant is more difficult since you must maintain the restaurant's atmosphere and avoid giving the impression that you are exercising excessive control. The Checkpoint Charlie mentality will not help your ambiance. In the dining room, you also must keep a close eye on the guests.

Cash registers are your basic security in front. They also are the point where a thief is most likely to hurt you. At the minimum, you will need to be able to account satisfactorily for departmental sales, cash and charge sales, sales tax, and bar receipts. A register capable of imprinting on a tape and on the guest check simultaneously will complicate a thief's day.

There are, of course, more complex systems able, it seems, to control a missile launch. Review your needs and select a system consistent with them. Yet even the most sophisticated register may be no match for a clever employee who wants to steal.

You pride yourself on the intelligence and initiative of your staff. Do not be surprised, then, if their methods of stealing are more inventive than Al Capone's. Following are three common techniques:

• The customer pays the exact amount of the bill, so the server or cashier does not ring up the sale but pockets the cash and guest check. Here, you will appreciate the importance of guest-check controls.

• The customer pays the check, but the employee underrings the amount and pockets the difference.

• The cashier operates with an open cash drawer. It is easy to forget to ring a sale.

To avoid these difficulties, it is important that all cash banks be counted at the beginning and end of each shift, that you control and count your guest checks, and that other control procedures be followed.

Some of your guests will steal if given the chance. Ashtrays go, of course, as do other small objects. But your rare antiques might have an appeal, as do coat trees, chairs, bottles of wine, photos, and food. Then, too, your employees may have friends who come to your restaurant to cheat you. If you do not have good controls, the friends can eat an entire meal, then leave without paying the check, which the server simply pockets.

Although many people maintain that a large percentage of people will steal if given a chance, I remain convinced that the most effective means of curtailing pilferage is through intelligent hiring, thorough training, and inspired supervision. The ability of an owner to create loyalty and trust is as much a function of attitude as pay scale. If employee needs are not considered, the rate of pay, no matter how high, begins to seem inadequate. Given that sort of dissatisfaction, it becomes easier for employees to justify the small thefts that seem common to restaurants.

This chapter has covered the innumerable details to be watched in a restaurant. I am not sure that the issue of security controls needs to be high on the list. The establishment of effective checks is your decision. Discuss it with your accountant and any-one else who will listen. A 600-square-foot family restaurant needs less rigid internal controls than a 10,000-square-foot monster em-ploying a hundred people. If you do not exact rigid obedience to the controls you establish, the entire system may be more hindrance than help. Think it through.

A book entitled *Honest Business*, by Micahel Phillips and Salli Rasberry (Random House, 1981), offers an intriguing approach to business practices for the small operator. The authors contend that the more open an owner is about all aspects of the business, the more likely employees are to feel a loyalty to that business. Of course, this is almost a self-fulfilling prophecy, since owners who are capable of openness and honesty are more likely to attract employees of similar character.

Shortly after Perry Butler opened Perry's in San Francisco, an emergency repair was necessary in one of the dining rooms. The problem occurred just as lunch was beginning. As a consequence, two lunch waiters who were already at work had no customers and no way to earn tips for the day. Perry donated money for the tips lost because of the repair work.

Georg Isaak has worked for many years at the Blue Boar in San Francisco. The restaurant's two partners include him in the management of the business. Georg handles most of the owners' correspondence. He has been paid the compliment of trust and returns it with his contributions to the restaurant.

Although I am not suggesting that you necessarily open your books to every employee nor become a foster home for vagabond waiters, I do believe that if you have an open approach to your staff, your trust will be returned.

Publicity and Advertising

Publicity is a vital element in your restaurant's growth, and it can take many forms.

In the late 1970s, Ed Moose of the Washington Square Bar & Grill in San Francisco organized and sponsored a baseball team composed of friends and patrons. This, in itself, is not particularly unusual. But Ed's team played only one game, in Paris, against a wine-consulting firm's team. The event was described in a long article in *Sports Illustrated*.

Most restaurant owners are aware that advertising is not nearly as effective as events that garner free publicity. You do not have to take teams to Paris. Local charity and community service may be easily as effective in your town. Ed notes that, "You can't make publicity. You have events. You make something happen."

Equally important to a restaurant's success is word-of-mouth publicity. People talk about food almost as much as they do about the weather. Everyone is interested in good places to eat. If your restaurant gains a reputation as a well-run, decent operation, your chances for success increase dramatically.

Beware the evil reputation. Recently, a new restaurant opened near my home; there was much publicity and quite extravagant claims of excellence. On my first visit, I was greeted by a young, enthusiastic but nervous waitress. I did not mind her lack of experience. I did mind the restaurant's tasteless food, which was more expensive than that served by a similar place nearby and less satisfying in its portions. My experience at the new place was confirmed by other people who, unasked, would mention similarly distasteful meals. That is a poor way to begin.

When buying advertising, consider a variety of media. Newspapers, radio stations, and telephone yellow pages are good possibilities. Many owners favor advertising in community business guides, programs for musical and dance events, or entertainment guides.

A metropolitan restaurant might never advertise in the city's newspaper but might buy space weekly in the symphony program. A small-town operation may appear in the community center's annual Christmas play program and also in the local paper, not necessarily because the newspaper is more effective, but because virtually everyone in town glances through the paper. Small-town businesses can be mutually beneficial. An advertising check to the newspaper brings free publicity later or perhaps regular lunch business from the newspaper's staff.

You must identify your audience and concentrate upon the distinguishing features of your restaurant. Throughout the construction phase of your place, you were continually trying to refine the ideas and goals of your restaurant. That process is no less important in selecting advertising.

Creative Growth

As your restaurant matures, you will want to inject new ideas and recipes into the menu to maintain quality and appeal. Many restaurant offices are stacked with practical cookbooks that are excellent sources of new recipes. Professional chefs who write those books place appropriate emphasis upon the freshness of the raw food and the most effective means of preparation, and their experiences can provide you with ideas and inspiration.

Several fine writers have approached food not simply as a nutritional product but in light of sensual, aesthetic, and intellectual considerations. For writers such as M. F. K. Fisher, Waverly Root, and Brillat-Savarin, the eating of food is more than the fulfillment of a physical need. Through food they discover relationships between the body's needs and the desires of the soul, between the individual and the world. Food becomes an aid to memory, a catalyst for thought. It is a practical source of nourishment and a dreamer's lure to reverie. You will discover in these writers a beautiful, sensitive awareness of the importance of food in every community.

9

Liquor Operations

In regard to inventory control, personnel management, and attention to detail, running an establishment with a liquor license is not markedly different from one that has only a beer and wine license. Yet certain characteristics of liquor operations are sufficiently peculiar to warrant further discussion.

In talking about liquor licenses in Chapter Two, we already touched upon several distinctive features and problems associated with this type of license. The daily activity in a bar can create surprises for the uninitiated.

Controlling Costs

People control will occupy much more of your time than inventory control. If you already have established an effective system to account for liquor bottles, you need not spend too many sleepless nights wondering how well that system is working. Liquor generally arrives in sealed, easily counted cases. It stores readily, and usually you will have no reason to be concerned about the consistency of its quality. Even though liquor bottles are relatively easy to steal, your regular inventory procedures coupled with a precise issuing routine will eliminate most difficulties.

Usually bar owners establish a par system for stocking the bar. A precise number of bottles of each brand is issued from the storerooms and stocked at the bar. All empty bottles are recorded at the end of the day on a break sheet. The total "broken" must agree with the number of replacements from storage.

After the liquor has reached the bar, it is still possible to maintain control. You are, of course, confronted with the need to balance atmosphere and conviviality with control and security. Many larger operations have liquor and soft drink dispensing systems that provide a measured amount of liquid. These pouring systems also can be tied into a cash register to automatically record the sale. Still, they cannot provide absolute control.

With a little added managerial effort and a little less paranoia, an effective manual system can be devised to provide good security while maintaining a sense of humaneness important to a comfortable saloon.

Your bar's cash register should be tailored to the needs of your operation. Naturally, you will want to account for all transactions. One method is to require that the bartender issue a bar check or tape receipt with every drink poured. That is one way to keep an eye on the money since the customer knows that a specified amount of money has been recorded in the machine.

Another method involves calculation of the revenue expected per day based upon the number of ounces of liquor sold. That anticipated amount is then compared with the actual sales figures. For instance, a vodka bottle containing thirty-two ounces and used to pour drinks of one-and-a-half ounces should yield twenty-one drinks. Based upon the selling price of your drinks, you can calculate what your sales amounts should be by pricing the total ounces of liquor sold at the sales price. If only two ounces remain in the vodka bottle at the end of the day and if drinks sell for $1.25 each, then you expect to have taken in $25.00 (20 drinks × $1.25 = $25.00). Of course, this method does not take into account the variations in drink prices. A Bloody Mary may bring in more revenue than a vodka on the rocks while still using the same amount of liquor.

You also might take a bar inventory at the end of each day. Thus, the exact amount of liquor poured is known for comparison with the total issued.

A system requiring managerial verification of each spill is needed. Mistakes or spills should be rung on a bar tab to account for all errors. A few ounces of liquor washed down your sink daily can have a drastic impact on pour costs. In *Food Equipment Facts*, Carl Scriven and James Stevens present shocking figures to demonstrate the dollars and stock lost per month through waste and overpouring. If an operator pours one-ounce shots, buys thirty cases (twelve bottles per case) of liquor per month, and loses two ounces per thirty-two-ounce bottle because of waste, then the equivalent of 22.5 bottles is wasted each month.

The authors also present a chart detailing the amount of revenue lost based upon retail sales. At $1.25 per ounce, two ounces per bottle wasted, and thirty cases per month purchased, the owner is losing $900 per month through waste. From this example, you can easily understand why many owners use a controlled-pour system in an attempt to reduce errors.

In many bars, the bartender is allowed to buy drinks for patrons. Within reason, this practice may not be detrimental, though many owners rightly demand that promotional drinks be approved by management and rung on a promo bar tab. Any drinks that do not bring in revenue still must be accounted for; otherwise they will distort the liquor pour costs.

The Bartender

Perhaps the most effective method of controlling liquor costs is to hire more selectively and train more thoroughly. Bartenders can be taught to pour correctly. They can be educated in the need for cost control and imbued with a spirit of cooperation.

As supervisor, you must watch closely when the bartender is pouring. Has the proper amount of liquor been added—neither too much nor too little, but the exact amount determined by the owner to constitute a balance between profit and pleasure? Is the money collected immediately, or does the bartender leave it on the bar hoping for a larger tip or a "sleeper"—a stack of bills inadvertently left by a departing customer? Is the bartender aware that many regular patrons prefer not to have stiff drinks? One of their purposes in drinking is to remain in the bar for a comfortable length of time. Usually they do not wish to be blasted off their stools with the first sip.

Bartenders have a reputation for dishonesty that places them in the ranks of bank robbers and politicians. Although suspicions about a bartender's honesty are not always unfounded, few proprietors have any reason to be critical.

In most individually owned restaurants, there is little need to worry about bogus bottles, shot glasses filled with resin, or brand switching. Undoubtedly, the most common form of theft occurs when the employee simply pockets the cash without ringing the sale. But since most people are honest, it is not likely that you will encounter many such tricksters.

There are more subtle ways for your bartender to hurt you. One Christmas season, after a tough day of shopping, I entered a bar and restaurant widely known for its general grooviness. All I wanted was a simple drink and a few moments alone. Although the bar was not busy, I could not get the bartender's attention. He was too busy chatting up the cocktail waitress. Her customers could not get drinks either.

The person responsible for hiring and supervising in that place was not performing well. Bartenders often are relied upon to oversee bar and cocktail operations. They should have the maturity and mentality to do the job. Because I left without buying a drink, that bartender had as effectively denied the owner revenue as if he had stolen from the till.

One of your bartender's primary responsibilities is the adroit handling of customers. In my opinion, at least 50 percent of a bartender's job is this very demanding art of responding to patrons' moods. Virtually anyone can be trained to pour drinks. It is the sensitivity to people's psychological and emotional needs that marks the good bartender.

Behind the bar, the bartender is on stage. Working becomes a performance. The presentation is always within arm's reach of the customer, who, like a theatre patron of several hundred years ago, is a participant also.

Even if you are not gregarious, it is important for you to recognize that quality in others. Cultivate it in your staff. Unlike the food server, who can retreat to the sanctuary of the kitchen, your bartender is penned in by the bar. People with a low tolerance for pressure should not be back there.

Dealing with Drunks

All your staff should be trained to identify and handle customers who have had a few too many drinks. The drunk can hurt you by driving away other customers or by getting you sued under the liquor liability laws.

People who are drunk can be very devious in their efforts to buy another drink. I have seen the obviously inebriated stand outside a place, breathing fresh air deeply and concentrating mightily with the last of their reserves. Having pulled themselves together, they march directly to the bar. Enunciating clearly, they ask for a drink. When the bartender asks them to repeat the order, they generally go to pieces. Unable to repeat the performance, they sag, their self-control shattered.

Your staff must always be alert for drunks. Many people can consume prodigious amounts and then, with the sip of that fatal ounce, be pushed over the edge into oblivion.

People who have had too much should be offered coffee and possibly an invitation to return another day (this helps to reduce antagonism). Say almost anything that will take their minds off alcohol. Only the most crazed drunks need to be muscled, and even then, not until they have gone beyond the bounds of civilized behavior. If your people are doing their jobs, your place should not be cursed with violent drinkers.

Daily Bar Operations

The setup procedures for a bar are no less important than in other restaurant areas. Generally, the process should not take too long. Cleanliness and orderliness should be emphasized. A typical routine might include the following:

Wipe down all shelves, sinks, and cabinets
Clean and fill fruit containers with lemon wedges, lemon twists, limes, onions, oranges, olives, and cherries
Clean and fill juice containers
Stock back-up fruits and juices
Stock bar with liquor, wine, beer, and soft drinks
Clean mixer and mixing cans

Set up pour trays, bar mops, ashtrays, matches,
  and condiments
Clean and stock all bar glasses

On a weekly basis, the ice bins should be emptied and cleaned, the reach-in boxes cleaned, and the back bar wiped down and polished. Also clean beer lines and taps.

Your selection of liquors, wines, and beers must be as careful as your choice of food products. Generally, you will find far fewer liquor distributors than food suppliers. Many have exclusive rights to specific liquors in their area, so you will not have to worry about choosing the best distributor.

If there is a wine-growing region nearby, you often can select from a wide variety of vineyards. Deliveries may be irregular, but at least the selection is there. For restaurants located far from wine-growing areas, the choice of wines is often limited and not always exciting.

If you are not knowledgeable about wine, be particularly careful when making up a wine list. Liquor sales reps can be helpful, but naturally they are interested in having their wines on your list. Without too much effort, your wine list could begin to look like an advertisement for a particular liquor supplier's line of wines.

Suppliers often hold training seminars or conduct tours for staff. Basic knowledge of wines, wine making, and liquors can be easily learned. It is information that will enhance your employees' work performance.

When you price your wine list, try to remember that frequently you will be serving a product that is identical to what your customer can find on his wine merchant's shelf. Some operators charge only a couple of dollars over their cost; others raise the price by three times the wholesale cost. Personally, I believe that making a couple of dollars on each bottle will cover handling costs. The benefit is not financial but is found in the enjoyment of the wine by customers who will appreciate your fairness and commitment to pleasant dining.

Like your food prices, your drink prices greatly influence your gross sales and the type of customers your place will attract. Most bar operators charge different prices for well drinks (the standard brands poured by the house), call brands (drinks specified by brand name when the customer orders), premium call, cognacs, cream drinks, and coffee drinks. The selling price can be determined in the same manner as food prices. Also try to keep prices compatible with your neighborhood and your competition.

On the other hand, the price of soft drinks and fruit juices in bars often bears no relation to their perceived value. Soft drinks actually may cost the restaurant the same price per ounce as beer. Few customers realize that fact. Even fewer employees, forever consuming soft drinks, comprehend their actual cost.

The wholesale price of soft drinks is not the sole reason for charging a high bar price for them. You are running a bar, not an ice-cream parlor. You want to sell liquor, not sugar water. You might charge the same price for a soft drink as for a beer to discourage soft-drink sales.

Some products need to be priced differently. For instance, it may be beneficial to mark up imported beer less than domestic products, thereby reducing the absolute profit on each bottle sold but increasing the number of sales and offering a more equitable pricing system for customers.

A well-run comfortable bar can be a definite asset to a restaurant. The owner must be very conscious of the customers and the atmosphere. Sensitivity to mood and a willingness to control every aspect of the operation can do much to maintain a civilized drinking establishment.

Daily operations in the dining room and bar require supervision of endless details. The smart restaurant owner knows that as long as customers continue to come through the front door, the supervisory work will happily continue. With more business, your job will become more complex and time-consuming. Your difficulties will increase with your sales. That is not an unhappy situation. As Michael McCourt observes, "When the cash register stops ringing, you've got real problems."

10

Moments Not Meals

Your restaurant will be a statement of your taste and your personality. It will reflect your character and your ideas. Despite the demands of time and effort, the operation will bring you joy and satisfaction. Since you will be working for yourself, the restaurant's standards of performance, integrity, and excellence will be yours alone. Within the limitations of budget, energy, and imagination, the restaurant will be you. As such, the complications of design and operation, quickly mastered and comparatively easy to maintain, will be less significant than the more subjective rewards derived from providing good, honestly prepared food for a reasonable price.

The preceding chapters were not intended to anger or to frustrate you. In every restaurant there are a thousand details needing attention. But a quick look at the restaurant operations in your community will soon convince you that mastery of the fundamentals requires no massive intellect.

It is easy to point out the restaurant operators who apparently disregard every precept of good business practice yet manage to keep their places open. Some even prosper. Others, blessed with good locations or without competition, can be irritatingly arrogant in their treatment of customers. Nevertheless, they function and may thrive.

More distressing are those restaurateurs who are obviously intent only upon making a fast dollar. They may invest millions in their operation, but their hype, their attitude, and the restaurant's atmosphere proclaim an operator who really has no respect for food or for the people in the restaurant.

That situation exists in all businesses. The dishonest auto repairman, the inept dentist, the unscrupulous attorney are all minorities who can give otherwise honorable professions a bad name. Unprincipled restaurant operators are no less tiresome. Nor are they always recognizable by the quality of their food which may be quite acceptable. Instead, it is the mannered arrogance, the lack of sensitivity, the overreaching pride which marks them as profiteers and exposes the meanness of their goals.

If you have had only limited experience in the restaurant business, the explanation of finances, planning considerations, and daily operations may have appeared overly complex. On the other hand, little of this material is as obscure as a tax return and none requires several college degrees to learn. Just as the restaurant is an accumulation of details, the knowledge of those details can be learned gradually.

For many readers, intent upon creating a small, personal restaurant, the intricacies of inventory management and cost analysis are not appropriate. For those topics and others relating to the restaurant business, use the information you find compatible with your style, disregard the remainder.

The need to explain the methods of business often leads inevitably to an undue emphasis upon everything which can go wrong. But what of the joys? The thousands of restaurateurs in this country are not all in the business solely because they enjoy pain. Apparently, they find other satisfactions.

For many operators, the primary pleasure—aside from monetary reward—is derived from the people they work with, from employees, customers, and other food industry workers. This is not to say that every individual will bring unfettered joy into your life. But the very nature of the business results in a close involvement with the inner lives of others.

As you have undoubtedly noted while reading through this book, I enjoy restaurant employees and find them, as a group, to be interesting, friendly, and generally a pleasure to be around. The following remarks by restaurant owners were made in response to my questions regarding the best aspects of owning a restaurant. Their words typify the personal benefits of restaurant ownership:

> "The best part of owning a restaurant is the satisfaction of seeing what all the employees can do together." (Guy Cardon; The Bluebird; Logan, Utah).

> "What typifies the joy and agony to us would probably be the growth of our personnel. Some of them grow, develop, and mature while working with and for other people." (Thomas Whitehead; Shamus McGregor's; Newport News, Virginia).

> "One of the best parts is seeing personnel develop. Of handing a young dishwasher his first paycheck." (Ned Foley; Steamer Gold Landing; Petaluma, California).

> "To help a teenage employee would be my greatest pleasure. A former employee burglarized the establishment and stole nearly $1,000. After a lot of personal detective work by yours truly (and the police), the person admitted the theft. It was decided after a payment plan was worked out not to prosecute. Today, this person is in a high position at a national restaurant chain and has won several awards for excellence from their firm." (Roger Kennedy; Three Pigs Barbecue; McLean, Virginia).

Like many other owners, these restaurateurs derive great satisfaction through their work with people. Nor are the pleasures restricted to contact with employees. The customers, too, are an endless source of surprise and fascination. In your restaurant, you will have all types, from the happy people who will be familiars after their first visit to the quiet ones, returning for weeks or months to sit unobtrusively through contemplative meals.

Sure, you have to earn a living, pay the rent, cough up your taxes. These annoyances apply to any business. The presentation of food, with its combination of physical properties and emotional and intellectual overtones, distinguishes a restaurant.

While opening a restaurant can be difficult, the business itself can be enormously rewarding in terms of individual accomplishment. You are foregoing the traditional allurements of guaranteed retirement plans and job security. This in itself can be of incalculable personal benefit. That willingness to gamble, to trust to your own strengths, yields greater self-confidence and a heightened sensitivity to the changes in your own life.

You will be faced with innumerable difficulties, yet the final result will be a physical expression of your particular vision. When you create your dream, you will have the joy which comes from individual achievement, and you will experience an increased sense of excellence and purposefulness within yourself.

To own and operate a restaurant is to participate in the private lives of your patrons. Because of the importance of food in human affairs and because of the relationship to food to celebration, to memory, to all aspects of daily life, your restaurant will become a catalyst, an intimate part of your community. For many of your customers, your place will be an integral part of their daily routine, an element in the fabric of their existence as significant in its way as their place of work.

The food and recognition you give to people is nourishment for their bodies and for their personalities. Your food, important in its own right as an expression of your best creative efforts, becomes a form of communication between customer and establishment. The food—its aroma, its texture, its taste—connects the restaurant—its decor, its employees, and its atmosphere—to those customers. The food is the bond and the basis of your relationship to your customers.

But food achieves its greatest importance when you serve it with a recognition of its intellectual and emotional meanings, when food becomes a gift in which you acknowledge that the customers have chosen your restaurant as a place to eat, to converse, to live for a few hours and that you understand the restaurant's importance to them not simply as a source of nourishment but as a part of their life.

To your customers, the time spent in your place may be as uneventful as a cup of coffee or laden with consequences effecting the subsequent course of their lives. Within the narrow walls of your restaurant, people will be participating in events which will remain in their memory long after the meal has ended. It is to your benefit and to theirs to recognize this dimension of the restaurant business. It cannot be quantified, for it is an intensely personal relationship which is fostered by your efforts and your customers' needs.

You may have patrons coming to your restaurant merely to eat your food. But many will have other reasons for visiting you which are as various as life itself: Parents may bring young children to the restaurant for one of the youngsters' first experiences in dining out; occasionally, people without a great deal of money may choose your place to celebrate a birthday or an anniversary on one of their infrequent evenings together—yours is an immense responsibility to provide them a pleasant, rewarding stay; your place may be one facet of a teenager's senior prom reminiscences; it may be a refuge, a sanctuary where daily problems are forgotten; it might be the scene of a marriage proposal or the site of a dinner celebrating a pregnancy, a birth, a marriage, or a day simple and productively concluded.

You, your employees, and your restaurant will be a portion of these people's experience. You are in the business of offering not only a tangible, physical product but a theater in which lives interact and dreams begin. You are, in short, creating not only meals but memories.

Appendix A

Food Service Equipment Directory

What is FEDA?

FEDA's origin dates from 1933 when a small group of the leading firms in the restaurant equipment business banded together as the Food Service Equipment Industry (FSEI) to protect their fledgling industry against unreasonable restrictions that might be arbitrarily imposed under the National Industrial Recovery Act (NRA).

Their initial efforts met with success. This set the pattern for the activist role the organization has played as FSEI until 1971, and Foodservice Equipment Distributors Association (FEDA) since then, in speaking for and representing distributors of foodservice equipment on government affairs as an association and through our affiiliation with the National Association of Wholesaler/Distributors. All members of FEDA are automatically members of NAW/D, which is recognized as one of the strongest and most effective government relations organizations in Washington.

FEDA is the only national association whose sole interest is representing and speaking for the distributor of foodservice equipment within the industry. Our activities in this capacity vary depending on the need, but whenever the need arises, FEDA will be there as spokesman for the foodservice distributor and in doing those things for our members that they cannot so easily do for themselves.

In addition, FEDA provides its members with an ever increasing list of benefits in various programs and services designed to enable them to operate more efficiently, effectively and profitably.

Although not all distributors of foodservice equipment are members of FEDA it is conservatively estimated that our membership accounts for 70% of the total dollar sales made in the industry through distributors.

Geographic Listing

ALABAMA
Birmingham
Foremost Food Facilities Corp.
(205) 328–7595
401 S. 28th St.,
Birmingham, AL 35233
Mobile
Mobile Fixture &
Equipment Co., Inc.
(205) 438–9712
308 St. Louis St.,
Mobile, AL 36601

ALASKA
Anchorage
E. L. Alaska Services
(907) 276–2616
1421 W. 56th Ave.,
Anchorage, AK 99503

Osky Supply Co., Inc.
(907) 274–8505
1700 Post Rd.,
Anchorage, AK 99501

ARKANSAS
Little Rock
Faucett's Equipment Co.
(501) 847–3587
9203 Hilard Springs Rd.,
Little Rock, AR 72209

Krebs Bros. Supply Co., Inc.
(501) 644–5233
1301 Westpark, Suite 2,
Little Rock, AR 72204

ARIZONA
Phoenix
Berry Losee Food Equipment
& Supply Co.
(602) 258–8394
811 N. 13th Ave.,
Phoenix, AZ 85007

Tucson
Ford Restaurant Supply
(602) 885–2345
5851 E. Speedway,
Tucson, AZ 85712

CALIFORNIA

Los Angeles
S. E. Rykoff & Co.
(203) 622–4131
761 Terminal St.,
Los Angeles, CA 90021

Sacramento
Finegold's Inc.
(916) 441–6931
2410 9th St.,
Sacramento, CA 95805

San Diego
R. W. Smith & Co.
(714) 234–2244
501 11th Ave.,
San Diego, CA 92101

San Francisco
Royal Supply Co., Inc.
(415) 626–1700
501 15th St.,
San Francisco, CA 94103

San Leandro
Food Service Equipment, Inc.
(415) 678–2922
710 E. 14th St.,
San Leandro, CA 94577

COLORADO

Denver
Carson's, Inc.
(303) 534–3126
1301 Wazee St.,
Denver, CO 80204

Restaurant Equipment Co.
(303) 477–1688
3400 Mariposa St.,
Denver, CO 80211

Stores Equipment Corp.
(303) 534–3201
1431 15th St.,
Denver, CO 80202

The York Equipment Co.
(303) 892–7166
5100 Fox St.,
Denver, CO 80216

CONNECTICUT

Bridgeport
Globe Equipment Co.
(203) 367–6611
3000 Dewey St.,
Bridgeport, CT 06605

Hartford
B. Golden & Sons, Inc.
(203) 525–5631
3324 Main St.,
Hartford, CT 06120

New Haven
Connecticut Bar &
Restaurant Supplies, Inc.
(203) 865–5123
400 Crown St.,
New Haven, CT 06506

Waterbury
Waterbury Store Fixture Co.
(203) 756–8031
24 Spring St.,
Waterbury, CT 06720

DELAWARE
Fenwick Island
Dale's Inc.
(302) 539–5453
Sunshine Plaza,
Fenwick Island, DE 19944

DISTRICT OF COLUMBIA
E. B. Adams Co.
(202) 332–8100
1612 U St., N.W.,
Washington, DC 20009

FLORIDA
Ft. Myers
Sterling Supply Co.
(813) 334–4264
2137 Fowler St.,
Ft. Myers, FL 33901

Hallandale
Restaurant Equipment
Brokers Co., Inc.
(305) 454–3300
2910 S.W. 30th Ave.,
Hallandale, FL 33009

Jacksonville
Barsco, Inc.
(904) 354–4448
1007 W. Bay St.,
Jacksonville, FL 32204

E. H. Thompson, Co.
(904) 737–7320
8230 Baycenter Rd.,
Jacksonville, FL 32216

Miami
General Hotel & Restaurant
Supply Corp.
(305) 885–8651
7300 N.W. 77 St.,
Miami, FL 33166

Pensacola
Pensacola Restaurant Supply
(904) 434–2231
401 S. Palafox,
Pensacola, FL 32575

Tampa
Food Service Equipment Co.
(813) 839–5341
A Div. of Morco Ind., Inc.
5105 S. Lois Ave.,
Tampa, FL 33681

GEORGIA
Atlanta
Atlanta Fixture & Sales Co., Inc.
(404) 455–8844
3185 N.E. Expressway,
Atlanta, GA 30341

Augusta
Norvell Fixture &
Equipment Co., Inc.
(404) 724–3501
1252 Reynolds St.,
Augusta, GA 30903

Forest Park
Food Service Equipment Co.
(404) 366–9750
A Div. of Morco Ind., Inc.
176 Forest Parkway,
Forest Park, GA 30050
Hdqtrs: Food Service Equipment
Co., Tampa, FL

Gainesville

Food Service Equipment
(404) 536–6051
Div. City Ice Co.
514 Main St.,
Gainesville, GA 30501

HAWAII
Honolulu

Hawaii Hotel &
Restaurant Supply, Inc.
(808) 341–8751
3015 Koapaka St.,
Honolulu, HI 96819

Honolulu Restaurant
Supply Co., Inc.
(808) 946–2105
2043 S. Beretania St.,
Honolulu, HI 96826

ILLINOIS
Bensenville

Holleb & Co.
(312) 595–1200
800 Supreme Dr.,
Bensenville, IL 60106

Chicago

A A Store Fixture Co., Inc.
(302) 733–4920
538 Milwaukee,
Chicago, IL 60622

A & R Equipment Sales, Inc.
(312) 829–9800
1141 W. Madison St.,
Chicago, IL 60607

Chicago Bar &
Restaurant Supply, Inc.
(312) 271–3600
1510 W. Lawrence Ave.,
Chicago, IL 60640

Herzog Store Fixture Co., Inc.
(312) 666–2600
1034 W. Madison St.,
Chicago, IL 60607

Lesco Supply Co.
(312) 568–3020
548 W. 119th St.,
Chicago, IL 60628

Marlinn Restaurant Supply Co.
(312) 247–6800
4500 S. Western Ave.,
Chicago, IL 60609

Novak Food Service Equipment
(312) 733–2530
1143 W. Madison,
Chicago, IL 60607

Lombard

Schweppe & Sons, Inc.
(312) 627–3550
376 W. North Ave.,
Lombard, IL 60148

Melrose Park

M. L. Rongo, Inc.
(312) 343–8820
4817 W. Lake St.,
Melrose Park, IL 60160

North Riverside

Edward Don & Co.
(312) 842–6006
2500 S. Harlem Ave.,
North Riverside, IL 60546

Rockford

Sun-Ray Fixture Co.
(815) 962–7753
2110 11th St.,
Rockford, IL 61108

Waukegan

Federal China & Supply Co.
(312) 623–1310
114-118 Washington,
Waukegan, IL 60085

Western Springs

International Integrated Ind., Ltd.
(312) 246–7847
1324 Hillgrove Ave.,
Western Springs, IL 60558

INDIANA

Evansville

Brucken Co., Inc.
(812) 423–4414
401 N.W. 4th St.,
Evansville, IN 47708

Indianapolis

G. V. Aikman Co., Inc.
(317) 353–8181
6312 Southeastern Ave.,
Indianapolis, IN 46203

CFS Continental
(317) 291–2020
4000 W. 62nd St.,
Indianapolis, IN 46268

Hoosier China & Equipment Div.
(317) 352–0491
7035 Brookville Rd.,
Indianapolis, IN 46239

IOWA

Cedar Rapids

Star Fixture Co.
(319) 364–3423
1005 Third Ave., S.W.,
Cedar Rapids, IA 52404

Davenport

Hockenbergs
(515) 323–3681
926 3rd St.,
Davenport, IA 52808
Hdqtrs: Hockenbergs,
Des Moines, IA

Tri City Equipment Co.
(319) 322–5382
527 W. 4th St.,
Davenport, IA 52801

Des Moines

Bolton & Hay, Inc.
(515) 265–2554
2701 Delaware Ave.,
Des Moines, IA 50316

Hockenbergs
(515) 243–3131
2300 Bell Ave.,
Des Moines, IA 50306

Sorensen Equipment Co., Inc.
(515) 283–1529
2012 Cottage Grove,
Des Moines, IA 50312

Sioux City

Interstate Restaurant Supply
(712) 252–0551
1801 Fourth St.,
Sioux City, IA 51101

Waterloo

Krensky Fixture Co.
(319) 234–0392
1941 Hawthorne Ave.,
Waterloo, IA 50702

KANSAS

Kansas City

Greenwoods, Inc.
(913) 262–1400
One Select Plaza,
Kansas City, KS 66103

KENTUCKY

Bowling Green

Southern Kentucky Restaurant
Supply & Equip. Co.
(502) 782–0606
505 U S 31 W. By-Pass,
Bowling Green, KY 42101

Louisville

Chef Ware, Inc.
(502) 585–5893
835 E. Main St.,
Louisville, KY 40206

LOUISIANA

Baton Rouge

Cayard's, Inc.
(504) 356–3534
4215 Choctaw,
Baton Rouge, LA 70805

New Orleans

Loubat Glassware & Cork Co., Ltd.
(504) 523–2811
510 Bienville St.,
New Orleans, LA 70130

Albert J. Ruhlman Corp.
(504) 891–3786
3434 S. Saratoga St.,
New Orleans, LA 70115

Shreveport

Buckelew's Food Service Equip. Co.
(318) 424–6673
1715 Spring St.,
Shreveport, LA 71166

MAINE

Portland

Edward J. Sullivan, Inc.
(207) 774–5877
161 Commercial St.,
Portland, ME 04111

MARYLAND

Baltimore

Atlantic Equipment Co.
(301) 426–4700
4511 Harford Rd.,
Baltimore, MD 21214

Ottenheimer Equipment Co.
(301) 466–3800
5703 Pimlico Rd.,
Baltimore, MD 21209

J. Norman Otto Co., Inc.
(301) 732–7430
3930 Fleet St.,
Baltimore, MD 21224

Resnick Store Fixture Co., Inc.
(301) 358–1414
6114 Reisterstown Rd.,
Baltimore, MD 21215

Beltsville

Gill Co., Inc.
(301) 937–0001
10501 Tucker St.,
Beltsville, MD 20705

Gill Marketing Co., Inc.
(301) 441–1330
5020 Sunnyside Ave.,
Beltsville, MD 20705
Hdqtrs: Gill Co., Inc.,
Beltsville, MD

Rockville

L. N. Hill Co.
(301) 770–4800
5030 Boiling Brook Parkway,
Rockville, MD 20852

Salisbury

Barrall Brothers, Inc.
(301) 749–9112
913 E. Church St.,
Salisbury, MD 21801

Page Huff, Inc.
(301) 749–1477
Northwood Dr.,
Salisbury, MD 21801

MASSACHUSETTS

Attleboro

Flagstaff Foodservice Co.
(617) 399–8000
One Venus Way,
Attleboro, MA 02703

Boston

H. M. Faust Co.
(617) 262–1820
601-603 Newbury St.,
Boston, MA 02215

S. E. Rykoff & Co.
(617) 254–0300
Morris Gordon & Son Div.
221 N. Beacon St.,
Boston, MA 02135
Hdqtrs: S. E. Rykoff & Co.,
Los Angeles, CA

Fall River

Highland Restaurant Supply
(617) 673–1822
829-835 Robeson St.,
Fall River, MA 02720

Holyoke

Holyoke Equipment Co., Inc.
(413) 536–7750
109 Lyman St.,
Holyoke, MA 01040

New Bedford

Colonial Restaurant &
Store Equip. Co.
(617) 993–0984
480 Union St.,
New Bedford, MA 02740

Newton Highlands

Boston Showcase Co.
(617) 965–1100
66 Winchester St.,
Newton Highlands, MA 02161

North Woburn

Atlantic Store Fixture Co., Inc.
(617) 935–4300
18 N. Maple St.,
North Woburn, MA 01801

Springfield

Kittredge Equipment Co., Inc.
(413) 788–6101
2155 Columbus Ave.,
Springfield, MA 01104

Woburn

S. S. Pierce Company
(617) 935–7900
Woburn Foodservice
10 Wildwood St.,
Woburn, MA 01801

MICHIGAN

Bay City

Kirchman Brothers Co.
(517) 892–3561
71 Midland St.,
Bay City, MI 48706

Benton Harbor

Atlas Restaurant Supply, Inc.
(616) 925–7055
1101 Pipestone Rd.,
Benton Harbor, MI 49022

Detroit

Canton China & Equipment Co.
(313) 925–3100
6309 Mack Ave.,
Detroit, MI 48207

Franco Food Equipment, Inc.
(313) 584–0013
15614 W. Warren,
Detroit, MI 48228

Great Lakes Hotel Supply Co.
(313) 962–9176
1961 Grand River,
Detroit, MI 48226

A. J. Marshall Co.
(313) 831–9450
4400 Cass Ave.,
Detroit, MI 48201

Escanaba

Hiawatha Chef Supply, Inc.
(906) 786–6621
400 N. Lincoln Rd.,
Escanaba, MI 49829

Ferndale

Gold Star Products, Inc.
(313) 548–9840
10777 Northend Ave.,
Ferndale, MI 48220

Flint

Clark's Store Fixtures, Inc.
(313) 239–4667
1830 S. Dort Hwy.,
Flint, MI 48503

Grand Haven

Bastian Blessing
(616) 842–7200
Foodservice Equipment Division
422 N. Griffin,
Grand Haven, MI 49417

Manting Equipment Co.
(616) 842–6180
700 Fulton St.,
Grand Haven, MI 49417

Grand Rapids

Douglas Bros., Inc.
(616) 459–9157
106 S. Division Ave.,
Grand Rapids, MI 49503

Kalamazoo

Bond Supply Co.
(616) 349–9763
Wigginton Div.
5231 Miller Rd.,
Kalamazoo, MI 49001

Stafford-Smith, Inc.
(616) 343–1249
3414 S. Burdick St.,
Kalamazoo, MI 49001

Pontiac

Oliver Supply Co.
(313) 682–7222
150 S. Telegraph Rd.,
Pontiac, MI 48045

Traverse City

Fivenson Food Equipment, Inc.
(616) 946–7760
324 S. Union St.,
Traverse City, MI 49684

MINNESOTA

Minneapolis

Harrison House Foodservice
(612) 542–1722
Monarch Institutional Foods
1420 Zarthan Ave.,
S., Minneapolis, MN 55440

Palm Brothers
(612) 871–2727
2727 Nicollet Ave.,
Minneapolis, MN 55408

St. Cloud

St. Cloud Restaurant Supply
(612) 252–2977
100 Roosevelt Rd.,
St. Cloud, MN 56301

MISSISSIPPI

Jackson

Food Service Equipment Co.
(601) 948–0373
A Div. of Morco, Ind., Inc.
535 Ford Ave.,
Jackson, MS 39209
Hdqtrs: Food Service Equipment
Co., Tampa, FL

Tupelo

Hudson Equipment Co., Inc.
(601) 844–6228
337 N. Spring St.,
Tupelo, MS 38801

MISSOURI

Joplin

Joe Harding, Inc.
(417) 624–3020
7th & Wall Sts.,
Joplin, MO 64801

Kansas City

Index Store Fixture Co.
(816) 842–9122
521 Main St.,
Kansas City, MO 64105

Jax Fixture & Supply Co.
(816) 842–4230
200 W. 5th St.,
Kansas City, MO 64105

National Store Fixture Co.
(816) 421–6564
2540 W. Pennway,
Kansas City, MO 64108

Rose Restaurant Supply Co., Inc.
(816) 221–1206
1110 Truman Rd.,
Kansas City, MO 64106

Smith St. John
(816) 221–7300
1518 Walnut,
Kansas City, MO 64108

St. Joseph

Sherman's Restaurant
Equip. & Supplies
(816) 232–1877
209 N. Third St.,
St. Joseph, MO 64501

St. Louis

Bensinger's
(314) 426–5100
A Div. of Allen Foods, Inc.
8543 Page Ave.,
St. Louis, MO 63114

Duke Manufacturing Co.
(314) 231–1130
2305 N. Broadway,
St. Louis, MO 63102

Ford Hotel Supply Co.
(314) 231–8400
814 N. Broadway,
St. Louis, MO 63102

Servco Equipment Co.
(314) 781–3189
3189 Jamieson Ave.,
St. Louis, MO 63139

Southern Equipment
(314) 481–0660
A McGraw-Edison Co., Div.
4550 Gustine Ave.,
St. Louis, MO 63116

Springfield

Ozark Restaurant Equipment Co.
(417) 865–8791
Div. Ozark Paper &
Janitor Supply, Inc.
313–315 South Ave.,
Springfield, MO 65806

NEBRASKA

Omaha

Hockenbergs
(402) 551–7051
6171 Grover St., Omaha, NE 68106
Heqtrs: Hockenbergs,
Des Moines, IA

NEW HAMPSHIRE

Manchester

Interstate Restaurant
Equip. Corp.
(603) 669–3400
37 Amoskeag St.,
Manchester, NH 03102

NEW JERSEY

Atlantic City

Stein's Hotel Supplies
(609) 348–4747
2218 Atlantic Ave.,
Atlantic City, NJ 08401

East Hanover

M & J Frank, Inc.
(201) 887–1040
29 Eagle Rock Ave.,
East Hanover, NJ 07936

Middlesex

Do-All-Craft, Inc.
(201) 356–4210
320 Lincoln Blvd.,
Middlesex, NJ 08846

Neptune

Shore Restaurant Equip. Co., Inc.
(201) 775–1147
1006 11th Ave.,
Neptune, NJ 07753

Newark

Combined Kitchen Equip. Co., Inc.
(201) 482–7019
393 Central Ave.,
Newark, NJ 07103

Hawthorne Supply Co.
(201) 484–5220
321 Central Ave.,
Newark, NJ 07103

NEW YORK

Albany

Lewis Equipment Co., Inc.
(518) 465–5252
450 N. Pearl St.,
Albany, NY 12204

Bedford Hills

B & C Smith, Inc.
(914) 939–8002
332 Adams St.,
Bedford Hills, NY 10507

Bronx

M. Tucker Food Service
Equip. Co., Inc.
(212) 893–8686
1260 Oak Point Ave.,
Bronx, NY 10474

Buffalo

Ruslander & Sons, Inc.
(716) 881–0030
18 Letchworth St.,
Buffalo, NY 14213

Chappaqua

Food Equipment Systems, Inc.
(212) 547–1150
1 King St.,
Chappaqua, NY 10514

Elmira

Wilson Store Equipment, Inc.
(607) 734–3638
610 S. Main St.,
Elmira, NY 14904

Elmsford

Westchester Restaurant
Supply, Inc.
(914) 592–5200
One Nepperhan Ave.,
Elmsford, NY 10529

Flushing

Admiral Craft Equipment Corp.
(212) 539–8700
131-05 Fowler Ave.,
Flushing, NY 11355

Horseheads

Hample Equipment Co.
(607) 739–3621
One Miracle Mile,
Horseheads, NY 14845

Liberty

Sabloff's, Inc.
(914) 292–4300
Route 52,
Liberty, NY 12754

New York City

Ackley Mutual Equip. Co., Inc.
(212) 964–8688
358 W. 18th St.,
New York, NY 10011

Acme Restaurant Supply Corp.
(212) 477–0375
293 Bowery,
New York, NY 10003

Anchor Equipment Co., Inc.
(212) 966–0120
520 Broadway,
New York, NY 10012

Bass & Bass
(212) 228–5120
265 Park Ave. S.,
New York, NY 10010

Cook's Supply Corp.
(212) 691–8880
151 Varick St.,
New York, NY 10013

H. Friedman & Sons, Inc.
(212) 254–9000
16 Cooper Square,
New York, NY 10003

Ideal Restaurant Supply Co., Inc.
(212) 674–5550
294 Bowery,
New York, NY 10012

Metro Foodservice Equipment
(212) 966–7812
121 Bowery,
New York, NY 10012

Town Food Service Equip. Co., Inc.
(212) 473–8355
351 Bowery,
New York, NY 10003

Niagara Falls

Rainbow Food Service Equipment
& Supply Corp.
(716) 238–8787
5650 Simmons Ave.,
Niagara Falls, NY 14304

Port Chester

Harris Restaurant Supply, Inc.
(914) 937–0404
25 Abendroth Ave.,
Port Chester, NY 10573

Queens Village

Elaine Products Company, Inc.
(212) 776–6000
208-22 Jamaica Ave.,
Queens Village, NY 11428

Syosset

Tassone Equipment Corp.
(516) 921–6400
130 Eileen Way,
Syosset, NY 11791

Yonkers

Abbot-Yonkers Restaurant
Supply Corp.
(914) 965–5750
68-70 Main St.,
Yonkers, NY 10701

William Lloyd, Inc.
(914) 476–7555
1200 Nepperhan Ave.,
Yonkers, NY 10703

H. Weiss Co., Inc.
(914) 963–1338
170 Ludlow St.,
Yonkers, NY 10705

NORTH CAROLINA

Apex

Bob Barker Equipment Co.
(919) 362–8417
123 N. Salem St.,
Apex, NC 27502

Asheville

Asheville Showcase & Fixture Co.
(704) 258–2221
57 Broadway,
Asheville, NC 28802

Rex Equipment Co., Inc.
(704) 274–4373
47 Brook St.,
Asheville, NC 28803

Carrboro

Kaplan Restaurant Supply, Inc.
(919) 967–6981
409 E. Main St.,
Carrboro, NC 27510

Greensboro

Cochran Restaurant Equip. Co.
(919) 288–1351
3000 Lawndale Dr.,
Greensboro, NC 27408

Raleigh

The Montgomery-Green Co., Inc.
(919) 828–9311
1420 S. Wilmington St.,
Raleigh, NC 27611

Wilmington

Jacobi-Lewis Co.
(919) 763–6201
622 S. Front St.,
Wilmington, NC 28401

Wilson

Whitely's Enterprises, Inc.
(919) 291–6600
2000 Highway 301 S.,
Wilson, NC 27893

NORTH DAKOTA

Fargo

Dakota Food Equipment, Inc.
(701) 232–4428
1802 First Ave.,
Fargo, ND 58102

OHIO

Cincinnati

Lauber, Inc.
(513) 542–9100
260 W. Mitchell Ave.,
Cincinnati, OH 45232

F. G. Schaefer Co., Inc.
(513) 861–5550
2145 Florence Ave.,
Cincinnati, OH 45206

Cleveland

S. S. Kemp & Co.
(216) 391–4650
4301 Perkins Ave.,
Cleveland, OH 44103

Columbus

Chakeres Ohio Food Fixture Co.
(614) 228–6531
532-548 N. High St.,
Columbus, OH 43215

Louis R. Polster Co.
(614) 224–2878
585 S. High St.,
Columbus, OH 43215

Dayton

General Fixture and Supply Co.
(513) 222–2020
22 Mead St.,
Dayton, OH 45402

Findlay

Findlay Equipment Sales, Inc.
(419) 422–4872
525 W. Main Cross St.,
Findlay, OH 45840

Toledo

Steger-Showel Co.
(419) 693–0571
421 Main St.,
Toledo, OH 43605

E. & T. Tokles, Inc.
(419) 241–1117
615 Monroe St.,
Toledo, OH 43604

Youngstown

Store Engineering Co.
(216) 744–0253
52 E. Myrtle,
Youngstown, OH 44507

OKLAHOMA

Oklahoma City

Curtis Equipment Co., Inc.
(405) 943–7650
3920 N.W. 39th Expressway,
Oklahoma City, OK 73112

Gardner Hotel Supply, Inc.
(405) 236–4671
1700 W. Main,
Oklahoma City, OK 73106

Tulsa

Heller's Food Equipment
(918) 939–2254
2242 E. 6th St.,
Tulsa, OK 74104

K. P. Restaurant Supply Co.
(918) 582–2167
230 E. First St.,
Tulsa, OK 74103

OREGON

Portland

Brodie Hotel Supply, Inc.
(503) 228–8481
1039 Northwest Glisan,
Portland, OR 97209
Hdqtrs: Brodie Hotel Supply,
Inc., Seattle, WA

PENNSYLVANIA

Erie

Arthur F. Schultz Co.
(814) 454–8171
939 W. 26th St.,
Erie, PA 16512

Harrisburg

Restaurant Equipment House Inc.
(717) 234–5075
2218 Susquehanna St.,
Harrisburg, PA 17110

Weiss Bros. Equipment, Inc.
(717) 238–5248
2980 Jefferson St.,
Harrisburg, PA 17105

McMurray

Curran-Taylor, Inc.
(412) 941–5610
351 S. Washington Rd.,
McMurray, PA 15317

Philadelphia

Erno Products Co.
(215) 627–7611
65 N. Second St.,
Philadelphia, PA 19106

National Products Co.
(215) 627–5000
113-131 N. Second St.,
Philadelphia, PA 19106

Star Metal Co.
(215) 365–3000
Div. J. P. Heilweil Ind., Inc.
4700 Island Rd.,
Philadelphia, PA 19153

Pittsburgh

William Delp, Inc.
(412) 281–1196
2211 Fifth Ave.,
Pittsburgh, PA 15219

Tyson Metal Products, Inc.
(412) 325–1200
1909 New Texas Rd.,
Pittsburgh, PA 15239

Scranton

W. P. Hoban Co.
(717) 343–5623
134 Franklin Ave.,
Scranton, PA 18503

State College

Jay Kay Distributors, Inc.
(814) 237–7618
1223 N. Atherton St.,
State College, PA 16801

Wyomissing

Singer Equipment Co., Inc.
(215) 376–4931
950 Woodland Rd.,
Wyomissing, PA 19610

Memphis

Sulkin-Tate, Inc.
(901) 458–2503
485 N. Hollywood St.,
Memphis, TN 38112

United Restaurant Supply Co.
(901) 396–1601
3092 Bellbrook Dr.,
Memphis, TN 38116

Nashville

Robert Orr/Sysco Food
Service Co.
(615) 383–7500
One Centennial Plaza,
Nashville, TN 37202

TEXAS

Austin

Austin Restaurant Supply Co.
(512) 472–1127
210 Neches St.,
Austin, TX 78701

Dallas

Huey & Philp
(214) 742–2461
1900 Griffin St.,
Dallas, TX 75202

El Paso

National Restaurant
Supply Co., Inc.
(915) 544–2121
320 W. San Antonio,
El Paso, TX 79901

Galveston

Adler's Fountain Supply Co., Inc.
(713) 762–9617
2101 Strand St.,
Galveston, TX 77550

Houston

Champion Restaurant Equip. Co.
(713) 747–4423
4321 Old Spanish Trail
Houston, TX 77021

Gardner Restaurant Supply Co.
(713) 223–4641
3313 McKinney Ave.,
Houston, TX 77023

Gerber's Restaurant Supply Co.
(713) 652–2021
2222 Pierce Ave.,
Houston, TX 77003

Houston Restaurant
Supply Co., Inc.
(713) 222–1208
1620 Congress,
Houston, TX 77002

San Antonio

Ace Mart Restaurant Supply Co.
(512) 224–0082
411 S. Flores,
San Antonio, TX 78204

Glasstov Cafe Hotel Supply
(512) 225–2789
724 S. Flores,
San Antonio, TX 78204

Tyler

Dennard Supply Co.
(214) 595–3721
408 N. Broadway,
Tyler, TX 75710

RHODE ISLAND

North Smithfield

United Restaurant Equip. Co.
(401) 769–3220
Route 146A,
N. Smithfield, RI 02895

Pawtucket

Excellent Coffee Co., Inc.
(401) 724–6393
259 E. Ave.,
Pawtucket, RI 02860

Providence

Jacob Licht, Inc.
(401) 331–9555
765 Westminster St.,
Providence, RI 02903

SOUTH CAROLINA

Easley

Owens-Rampey, Inc.
(803) 859–1516
108 N. First St.,
Easley, SC 29640

Greenville
Food Equipment Co., Inc.
(803) 288–3737
Ketron Court,
Greenville, SC 29602

TENNESSEE
Bristol
Bristol Supply & Equip. Co.
(615) 764–5191
200-210 State St.,
Bristol, TN 37620

Chattanooga
Lilie-McCall
(615) 622–2197
1300 McCallie Ave.,
Chattanooga, TN 37404
Hdqtrs: Food Service Equipment,
Div. City Ice Co.,
Gainesville, GA

Knoxville
Heleco, Inc.
(615) 525–3661
718 Depot Ave.,
Knoxville, TN 37917

Scruggs, Inc.
(615) 637–2525
3011 Industrial Parkway E.,
Knoxville, TN 37921

UTAH
Salt Lake City
W. H. Bintz Co.
(801) 363–5821
423 W. 3rd S.,
Salt Lake City, UT 84110

Moore Supply Co.
(801) 487–1671
3000 S. Main St.,
Salt Lake City, UT 84115

Restaurant & Store Equip. Co.
(801) 364–1981
144 W. Third S. St.,
Salt Lake City, UT 84110

VIRGINIA
Alexandria
LeBow Restaurant
Equip. Co., Inc.
(703) 549–0020
1180 Pendelton St.,
Alexandria, VA 22314

Norfolk
Atlantic Equipment Corp.
(804) 853–6711
Princess Anne & Ingelside Rds.,
Norfolk, VA 23509

Richmond
John G. Kolbe, Inc.
(804) 644–4601
1605 Brook Rd.,
Richmond, VA 23220

Roanoke
Eastern Sales & Equipment
Service Corp.
(703) 362–1848
5231 Peter's Creek Rd. N.W.,
Roanoke, VA 24012

Swartz & Co., Inc.
(703) 343–4483
421 Luck Ave.,
Roanoke, VA 24002

Virginia Beach

Sandler Foods
(804) 464–3551
1224 Diamond Springs Rd.,
Virginia Beach, VA 23455

WASHINGTON

Everett

Bargreen Coffee Co.
(206) 252–3161
2821 Rucker, Everett, WA 98201
Hdqtrs: Bargreen Restaurant
Equip. Co., Seattle, WA

Mount Vernon

Bargreen's of Mt. Vernon, Inc.
(206) 336–5721
1321 Railroad Ave.,
Mt. Vernon, WA 98273

Seattle

Bargreen Restaurant Equip. Co.
(206) 682–1472
1275 Mercer,
Seattle, WA 98109

Brodie Hotel Supply, Inc.
(206) 223–7700
2300 Elliott Ave.,
Seattle, WA 98121

Spokane

Brodie Hotel Supply, Inc.
(509) 838–3181
East 402 Sprague St.,
Spokane, WA 99202
Hdqtrs: Brodie Hotel Supply,
Inc., Seattle, WA 98121

WEST VIRGINIA

Charleston

Capitol Restaurant Equip. Co.
(304) 343–7693
Div. of Midwest Corp.
518 Capitol St.,
Charleston, WV 25301

Clarksburg

Stone & Thomas, Inc.
(304) 624–7471
Commercial Division
222 W. Main St.,
Clarksburg, WV 26301

WISCONSIN

Madison

Kessenich's Ltd.
(608) 249–5391
131 S. Fair Oaks Ave.,
Madison, WI 53704

Messner, Inc.
(608) 256–0695
1326 E. Washington Ave.,
Madison, WI 53701

Milwaukee

F. W. Boelter Co., Inc.
(414) 645–2050
1136 W. National,
Milwaukee, WI 53233

Kiefer Corp.
(414) 342–8820
2202 W. Clybourn St.,
Milwaukee, WI 53233

Modern Cabinet &
Rest. Supply, Inc.
(414) 273–5582
507-509 W. Juneau Ave.,
Milwaukee, WI 53203

Wausau

CTL Co., Inc.
(715) 845–8281
1710 W. Stewart Ave.,
Wausau, WI 54401

WYOMING

Casper

Redman Supply Co., Inc.
(307) 265–0251
7020 Salt Creek Hwy.,
Casper, WY 82601

BERMUDA

Hamilton

Gilbert Darrell Store Equip., Ltd.
(809) 292–5340
DunDonald St.,
Hamilton, Bermuda

CANADA

Alberta

Bridge Brand Food Services, Ltd.
(403) 273–5151
1803 Centre Ave., N.E.,
Calgary, Alberta T2E 0A6

British Columbia

Northwest Restaurant &
Hotel Supply Ltd.
(604) 873–3871
2210 Cambie St.,
Vancouver, BC V52 2T7

Ontario

Restaurant Equip.& Supply Co.
(519) 438–2991
234 William St.,
London, Ontario N6B 3B9

Ideal Food Service Equip.
(416) 920–1411
459 College St.,
Toronto, Ontario M6G1A3

DOMINICAN REPUBLIC

Coditeca, C. Por A
(809) 533–2540
Calle 9 Esq. Calle 2,
Ens. El Cacique
Dominican Republic 299-2

PUERTO RICO

John Napoli &Associates
(809) 724–2929
308 Ponce De Leon Ave.,
San Juan, PR 00901

VIRGIN ISLANDS

Services, Inc.
(809) 773–7272
Sion Farm Commercial Center,
Farmsted, St. Croix 00840

Additional Members Not Listed Geographically

Sanitary Ice Systems
1815 Hospital Drive
Jackson MS 39204
Phone: (601) 373–0401
J. K. Oates, President

Bill Green Supply, Inc.
223 West Washington
Marquette, MI 49855
Phone (906) 226–8627
Dick Flack, President

Ablah Hotel Supply
800 East 11th Street
Wichita, KS 67214
Phone: (316) 262–1827
Amil Ablah, President

Food-Tech Systems, Inc.
4721 Augusta Road
Greenville, S.C. 29605
Phone: (803) 277–1315
Will F. Poston, Jr. President

Foodservice Products, Lts.
Brittons Cross Road
St. Michael, Barbados WI
David Mayers, President

A'la Carte Sales Company
16 Westview Road
West Caldwell, NJ 07006
Phone: (210) 678–1935
Albert Repoli, President

Waco Hotel Supply Co., Inc.
P.O. Box 7933
Waco, TX 76710
Phone: (817) 772–8600
W. C. Scheel, President

Louis Kaplan Rest. Eqpt. Inc.
250 Lafayette Street
New York, NY 10012
Phone: (212) 431–7300
Salvatore Sabella, Sr. President

Koplan Kitchens, Inc.
1018 W. Ashby Place
San Antonio, TX 78212
Phone: (512) 734–5049
Maynard D. Koplan, President

Gerde Institutional Foodservice
P.O. Box 61028
New Orleans, LA 70161
Phone: (504) 733–5200
Karl Pfefferle

Dykes Restaurant Supply Inc.
1217 Jordan Lane N.W.
Huntsville, AL 35805
Phone: (205) 837–1107
C. H. Dykes, President

Richardson Fixture Co.
445 East Cedar, Box 106
Gladwin, MI 48624
Phone: (517) 426–4481
Dick Schwager, President

Newman Fixture Company, Inc.
606 West Gaines P.O. Box 543
Monticello, AR 71655
Phone: (501) 367–6218
Robert E. Newman, President

Lady Baltimore Foods, Inc.
1601 Fairfax Trafficway
Kansas City, KS 66115
Phone: (913) 371–8300
Louis Fehr, Manager

Resco Restaurant Supply
960 South Virginia Street
Reno, NV 89502
Phone: (702) 786–6565
Paul Oelsner, President

Dixie Eqpt. Co.
701 East Collins
Little Rock, AR 72202
Phone: (501) 372–2205
Vernon Rodgers, President

Bargreen-Ellingson Inc.
6626 So. Sprague
Tacoma, WA 98409
Phone: (206) 475–9201
Paul Ellingson, President

Smith & Green Company
407 Dexter Avenue N.
Seattle, WA 98109
Phone: (206) 682–2611
James Smith, President

Queen City Restaurant Eqpt. Inc.
2450 Seneca Street
Buffalo, NY 14210
Phone: (716) 826–3357
Leo Bukowski, President

Columbia Restaurant & Bar Spl
(Formerly E. L. Alaska)
1421 W. 56th Avenue
Anchorage, AK 99503
Phone: (907) 276–2616
Roy Devincenzi, President

Daytona Hotel &
Motel Supplies Inc.
401 South Atlantic Avenue
Daytona Beach, FL 32018
Phone: (904) 258–5350
Ernest L. Perri, MD, President

Superior Products
520 West County Road
New Brighton
St. Paul, MN 55112
Phone: (612) 636–1111
R. Ziegler, President

Willoughby Sheet Metal Co., Inc.
2210 W. Morris Street
P.O. Box 21006
Indianapolis, IN 46221
Phone: (317) 638–2381
Timothy Willoughby, President

Northwest Hotel Supply Co. Inc.
403 NW 9th Avenue
Portland, OR 97209
Phone: (503) 224–3420
Robert Rogers, President

Lindy's Restaurant Supply Co.
1515 N.W. Ballard Way
Seattle, WA 98107
Phone: (206) 783–2688
Lindy Powell, President

Dealer Food Service Eqpt.
2645 Linwood
P.O. Box 3071
Shreveport, LA 71103
Phone: (318) 222–9533
Sammy Pedro, President

Bar Boy Products, Inc.
250 Merritts Road
Farmingdale, NY 11735
Phone: (516) 293–7155
Edward DeFelice, Sr. President

Empire Food Service Eqpt. Corp.
200 Lafayette Street
New York, NY 10012
Phone: (212) 966–6620
Sheldon Lewis, President

Byczek Equipment Co.
3924 W. Devon Avenue
Chicago, IL 60659
Phone: (312) 673–6050
J. L. Byczek, President

North Shore Equipment Co.
P.O. Box 456
Round Lake, IL 60073
Phone: (312) 546–2267
Gus Karabetsos, President

Whitlock-Dobbs Inc.
2260 Marietta Blvd.
Atlanta, GA 30318
Phone: (404) 351–4211
Ralph W. Whitlock, President

Ft. Smith Restaurant Supply Co.
930 So. Phoenix
Ft. Smith AR 72901
Phone: (501) 646–1606
Robert R. (Bob) Marley Sr.
President

Kirby Restaurant
Supply Company
809 So. Eastman Rd. PO Box 8187
Longview TX 75607
Phone: (214) 757–2723
Thomas Bell President

Metro Restaurant Supply
1115 E. Harrison Avenue
Arlington, TX 76011
Phone: (817) 469–1221
Mack Duckett, President

Richard's Restaurant & Lounge
99 Verret Street
Houma, LA 70361
Phone: (504) 868–9240
Henry J. Richard, President

Sohn Supply Co.
P.O. Box 665
Houghton Lake, MI 48629
Phone: (517) 422–3522
Richard D. Follrath, President

Northern Restaurant Supply Co.
220 S. Michigan Ave.
Gaylord, MI 49735
Skip Kaiser, President

Howard Arnold Inc.
26 Crown Street
New Haven, CT 06507
Phone: (203) 787–2221
James Bianchi, President

Trenton China & Pottery
105 N. 2nd Street
Philadelphia, PE 19106
Louis Eidelson—President
Phone: (215) 627–1268

Soo Supply & Eqpt.
Orlando Pingatore
224 E. Portage
Sault Ste. Marie, MI 49783

Texas Hotel & Restaurant
3340 S. Jones
Ft. Worth, TX 76110
Curtis Cargo, President
Phone: (817) 921–6146

F.D. Stella Products Co.
7000 Fenkell
Detroit MI 48238
Phone: (313) 341–6400
F. D. Stella President

Acme Restaurant Supply
P.O. Drawer I
Charleston, SC 29402
Phone: (803) 723–9806
Bernice B. Silver, President

Hotel & Restaurant Supply
P.O. Box 6 Hwy. 39
Meridian, MA 39301
Phone: (601) 482–7127
P. B. Greene President

Restaurant Equipment Co.
925 W. Adams Box 10727
Jacksonville, FL 32207
Phone: (904) 356–0272
Raphael Klepper, President

Food Equipment Specialists
2525 Murworth Suite 200
Houston TX 77054
Phone: (713) 660–8959
Sanford E. Manning

Harbour Food Service
Equipment
119 W. Washington St.
Boston, MA 02114
Phone: (617) 227–8300
Phillip Kalick, President

Austin Drink & Food
Equipment Co.
Division of Austin
Carbonic Co., Inc.
501 E. 3rd
Austin, TX 78701
Phone: (512) 476–4693
Jack Brandes

Greg Restaurant
Eqpt. & Supplies, Inc.
112 North Street
Burlington, VT 05401
Phone: (802) 864–6813
Roland Gregoire, President

Germain Restaurant & Bar
Equipment Co., Inc.
208 Straight St.
Paterson, NJ 07505
Phone: (201) 742–1870
Stephen A. Rosen, Vice President

Zeta Food Service Equipment
& Design, Lts.
1695 Park Drive
Traverse City, Michigan 49684
Phone: (616) 947–7660
Bruce A. Muzzarelli, President

Appendix B
Useful Forms

The forms included in this appendix are not intended to be all-inclusive, or even precisely geared to your particular business. They are merely to give you an idea how certain functions are recorded and followed. By looking at these forms, you should be able to devise similar ones that will work for you.

Meat, Seafood, Poultry
Order Sheet

Item	Description	Co.	Build	On hand	Order	✔
Prime rib	112 rib eye 2" lip					
N.Y. strip	9" 3 × 2 selected					
Flank	trimmed					
Ham	EZ cut water added					
Salami	3-lb roll					
Bacon	16–18 lb					
Canadian bacon	roll					
Pork sausage	2-oz patties					
Ground meat	bag					
Top round	whole					
Petrale sole	fresh or frozen					
Mahi mahi	fletch					
Clams	Little-Neck					
Bay shrimp	Marveless					
Crab meat	Dungeness					
Prawns	U 31–36					
Scallops	Medium					
Snapper						
Calamari	Ocean Garden # 5					
Salmon	8–10 lb fresh or frozen					
Lobster	Australian tails 8–10					
Chicken breasts	1 lb whole					
Blueberries						
Spinach	Chopped					
Orange juice	Frozen					
Strawberries	# 30 frozen					
Sword	Wheel					
Special						
Catch						

Dinner Preparation Sheet

Item	Amount forward	Prep.	Total build	Closing counts	Dinner counts
Combo					
Calamari					
Scallops					
Thermidor					
Snapper					
Gold sp.					
N.Y.					
London					
Prine					
Lge. cut					
Union					
Teri. ch.					
Pet. sole					
Mahi					
Salmon					
Swordfish					
Lobster					
Oscar					
Clams					
Catch/day					

Liquor and Wine Breakage

Manager/Bartender

_____   _____

	Breakage	Replace	Short	Breakage	Replace	Shor
Bourbon			Triple Sec			
Scotch			Kahlua			
Gin			Lt Menthe			
Vodka			Dk Menthe			
Rum			Lt Cacao			
Brandy			Dk Cacao			
Tequila			Tull. Dew			

everage Inventory (ine)

Location _____ Date _____ 19____

Entered by _____ Priced by _____ Extended by _____ No ___ of ___

Description	Storeroom	Service bar	Bar	Total	Price	Extentions
H. Gamy Beau.						
ringer Cab. Sauv.						
ringer Cab. Sauv.*						
utherford Cab. Sauv.						
tter Home Zin.						
tzer Petite Syrah						
B. Pinot Noir						
ondavi Pinot Noir						
ondavi Pinot Noir*						
othschild St. Emil.						
eaulieu Chablis						
B. Fumé Blanc						
ringer Chardonnay						
B. Pinot Chard.						
ente Grey Reisling						
ente Grey Reisling*						
enwood Chenin Blanc						
eb. Green Hungar.						
utherford P.N. Blanc						
eyser Peak Gewurzt.						
. Mich. Semillion						
. Mich. Johan. Rei.						
bisset Blanc						
nestet Graves Ex.						
ondavi Gamy Rose						
ondavi Gamy Rose*						
eaulieu Beaurose						
ancers Rose						
orbel Brut Champ.						
orbel Brut Champ.*						
omaine Chandon						
ouse Wine—Geyser Peak						
ouse Champagne						

Manager Schedule

Restaurant: _____

Dates: _____

Week of:	Mon.	Tues.	Wed.	Thurs.	Fri.	Sat.	Sun
Open							
Lunch float							
Dinner float							
Close							
Off							
3 dayer or vac.							
Mgr. trainee							

Appendix C
Additional Reading

Albers, Carl H. *Food and Beverage Cost Planning and Control Procedures.* East Lansing, Michigan: Educational Institute of the American Hotel Association, 1974.

Avery, Arthur C. *A Modern Guide to Food Service Equipment.* Boston: CBI Publishing Company, Inc. An excellent survey of restaurant equipment and its uses from a publishing company which produces many informative books dealing with the restaurant business.

_____. *The Best of Gottlieb's Bottom Line: A Practical Profit Guide for Today's Foodservice Operator.* New York: Lebhar-Friedman Books, Chain Store Publishing Corporation, 1980. A fine anecdotal guide for the daily operations of restaurants from another publishing company with extensive books devoted to foodservice.

Bolhuis, John L., and Wolff, Roger W. *The Financial Ingredient in Foodservice Management.* D. C. Heath and Company, 1976. Very direct and informative.

Child, Julia, and Beck, Simone, and Bertholle, Louisette. *Mastering the Art of French Cooking.* New York: Random House, 1961.

Cunningham, Marion, with Laber, Jeri, *The Fannie Farmer Cookbook.* Revised. New York: Alfred A. Knopf, 1979.

Dukas, Peter. *How to Plan and Operate a Restaurant.* Second Revised Edition. Rochelle Park, New Jersey: Hayden Book Company, Inc., 1973. A very useful book about the basics of restaurants.

Fisher, M. F. K. *The Art of Eating.* New York: Random House, 1976.

Friedlander, Mark P. Jr., and Gurney, Gene. *Handbook of Successful Franchising.* New York: Van Nostrand Reinhold Company, 1981. A very complete guide to the franchising business.

Green, Eric F., *et al. Profitable Food and Beverage Management Planning.* Rochelle Park, New Jersey: Hayden Book Company, Inc., 1978. A comprehensive guide to restaurant management. Contains a good bibliography.

Miller, Daniel. *Starting a Small Restaurant.* Boston: Harvard Common Press, 1978.

Mooney, Sean, with Green, George. *Sean Mooney's Practical Guide to Running a Pub.* Nelson-Hall, 1979.

Phillips, Micahel, and Rasberry, Salli. *Honest Business.* New York: Random House, 1981. Contains provocative ideas for organizing a business.

Penington, Jean A. T., and Church, Helen Nichols. *Bowes & Church's Food Values of Portions Commonly Used.* New York: Harper & Row, 1980.

Root, Waverly. *Food: An Informal Dictionary.* New York: Simon & Schuster, 1980.

Rombauer, Irma S., and Becker, Marion Rombauer. *Joy of Cooking.* Indianapolis, Indiana: Bobbs-Merrill, 1975.

Scriven, Carl, and Stevens, James. *Food Equipment Facts.* Troy, New York: Conceptual Design, 1980. An extremely useful guide to virtually every facet of the food business.

_____. *Small Business Reporter: Restaurants*. San Francisco: Bank of America. Thin but thorough study of restaurant planning. There is also a booklet on franchising in this series.

Stokes, John W. *How to Manage a Restaurant or Institutional Food Service*. 3rd edition. Dubuque, Iowa: William C. Brown Company Publishers, 1977. A very detailed work with primary application to larger operations.

Van Kleek, Peter E. *Beverage Managing and Bartending*. Boston: CBI Publishing Company, Inc., 1981.

Magazines

"Bon Appétit" by Bon Appetit Publishing Company; 5900 Wilshire Blvd., Los Angeles, CA 90036.

"Cornell Quarterly" by Cornell University School of Hotel Administration; Cornell University, Ithaca, NY 14853.

"Gourmet" by Gourmet, Inc.; 560 Lexington Avenue, New York, NY 10022.

"Nation's Restaurant News" by Lebhar-Friedman; 425 Park Avenue, New York, NY 10022.

"NRA News" by National Restaurant Association; 311 First Street N.W., Washington, D.C. 20001.

"Restaurants and Institutions" by Cahners Publishing Company; 5 S. Wabash Avenue, Chicago, IL 60603.

"Restaurant Business" at 633 Third Avenue, New York, NY 10017.